GROWING HERBS

Dawn Dunn

CASSELL

Dedication

This book could not have been written without the unselfish
love and whole-hearted support of my husband and our children.
To them I say thank you.

Publisher's Note: References in this book to the use of medicinal herbs are for
interest and general information only. Anyone suffering from ailments, internal or
external, are advised to consult a registered medical herbalist or qualified physician. Although herbs can most certainly cure, they can also kill in the wrong
hands, which is why self-diagnosis and treatment is not recommended. The author
and publisher accept no responsibility for adverse reactions or conquences that
may arise from the mis-use of any herbs mentioned in this book.

Reference: The botanical references used for this book were *Hortus Third*,
Macmillan Publishing Company, New York, 1976 and *The New RHS Dictionary
Index of Garden Plants*, Mark Griffiths (ed.), Macmillan, London, 1994.

Cassell Publishers Limited
Wellington House, 125 Strand
London WC2R 0BB

First published in Great Britain in 1997
in association with
David Bateman Limited
30 Tarndale Grove, Albany Business Park, Albany,
Auckland, New Zealand

Distributed in the United States by Sterling Publishing Co. Inc.,
387 Park Avenue South, New York, NY 10016, USA

British Library Cataloguing in Publication Data
A catalogue record for this book is available from the British Library

ISBN 0-304-34837-6

Photographs by Dawn Dunn
Printed in Hong Kong by Colourcraft Ltd

Biennial clary sage *Salvia sclarea*

Contents

INTRODUCTION

Nasturtium *Tropaeolum majus*

PEOPLE everywhere are interested in herbs. Some have a fleeting romance with exotic culinary herbs, others a life-long commitment to their use, but all have experience of these pleasing plants. Think of lamb with mint sauce, sage and onion stuffing and scrambled eggs with parsley or chives, and you come to realise just how much experience you have had with herbs. The most popular are the culinary herbs of which six are widely used — parsley, sage, thyme, chives, mint and garlic. But the range of herbs is vast and delights galore await those who are willing to explore this wonderful world.

Herbs excite, soothe, comfort, cure and delight. If you allow them, they bring a power and a magic to life in the form of sweet scents and full flavours. And there's that other dimension, the one you can't touch but can feel when handling herbs, a sense of times past and your place in history. And the more you learn about herbs the more enchanting and haunting they become as you discover how useful and important they have been to people through the ages.

Growing herbs delights almost all your senses — sight, smell, touch and taste. For your sight, some of the most beautiful garden plants are classified as herbs — roses, for instance. For the rest of your senses you need only work a while in a herb garden, brush against a bush of lemon verbena and, in the lemon-laden air, stoop to caress a lamb's ear or chew on a sprig of mint.

My earliest memories go back to pre-school days, playing in the mint patch by the dripping back door tap. It seemed to me that everyone grew mint beneath the outside tap when I was a child. And what a perfect place

This wonderful mixed herb border features biennial clary sage, left, lavender in the foreground and the sometimes invasive Queen Anne's lace at front right.

for mint it was, nice and damp. I can vividly see my mother picking sprigs to make mint sauce for the Sunday leg of lamb. Leftover leaves would be crushed and left on the kitchen window-sill to discourage flies. Then a clove of garlic would be cut into slivers and inserted in slits made in the meat while she reminded me that it was to garlic that I owed my good health. Finally, a bunch of parsley would be quickly and expertly chopped up to sprinkle on the carrots. Herbs played an integral part at our meal times.

After I was married we moved into a ground floor apartment where I could hardly wait to plant my first herb garden. In a sunny spot beside the back door I put in chives, parsley, sage and thyme together with lettuces and little gourmet tomatoes. Being busy working full time, and socialising when not at work, meant that the herb garden largely took care of itself. But I watched fascinated as the herbs produced flowers: lilac pom poms appeared in the midst of the clump of chives, there were lacy white brides' bouquets atop the parsley, brilliant blue spires on the sage bush and the thyme became a carpet of pink.

Not to be outdone, the lettuces bolted to their full height and looked very impressive between the trusses of sweet red tomatoes. I didn't get to use most of what I planted that year but I learned a lot about their lives.

As we travelled and lived in various countries around the world I always made sure I had pots of herbs on window-sills throughout the house. Somehow they instantly turned a house into a home.

In a corner of the bathroom I would place the mint where it got plenty of moisture, while the sunniest sills were reserved for the thyme and sage. Semi-shaded spots housed parsley pots and once we discovered Italian food, oregano and basil joined our family of herbs. Herbs indoors will always play second fiddle to a healthy outdoor garden, but it did-

n't seem to matter that the plants never developed to their full potential. The sight and smell were enough while they lasted, and they could always be readily replaced.

When we finally settled in suburbia to raise a family, the first 'real' herb garden was planted. Eagerly I put in as many herbs as I knew at that time, with little attention to spacing or design. I just wanted the herb patch to be a mass of mingled leaves and flowers, crowded and jostling like main city streets. I was soon to learn that some plants object to this treatment and watched in horror as the sage completely collapsed, parsley grew long and leggy, thyme disappeared,

savory never actually appeared and rosemary flattened anything else in its path. The important lesson here was that herbs, like most plants, like air to breathe and space to develop their natural shape.

Subsequent gardens taught me about good drainage, too much sun, too little sun, nutrients, wind, frost and little tricks like removing buds to prolong the use of leaves.

The most successful herb gardens for me have been raised ones, which confirms the fact that good drainage is a plant's best friend. Even moisture-lovers like mint and lemon grass grow well in a well-drained situation providing their water needs are taken

Herbs blend effectively into many garden designs. This appealing border includes lambs' ears, bergamot, curry plant, marjoram, rosemary and lady's bedstraw.

care of. As my library of herb books grew and essential reading at bedtime became herb magazines, I spread my wings and tried to grow every herb I read about. Not all were successful by a long shot, but I have had hours of pure pleasure learning and dreaming while watching and using those wonderful plants known as herbs.

Chapter 1

HISTORY

Angelica *Angelica archangelica*

LONG before humans learned to hunt animals, they foraged for food among the plants, roots, berries and herbs. Life depended on plants and as they flourished through the seasons so did people, moving from place to place as the plants, including herbs, produced their bounty. The availability of edible plants and herbs played an increasingly important part in our survival and well-being. As grains became a major part of the diet, herbs were given the added role of flavour enhancers.

The earliest written records on the use of herbs are to be found among the papyrus scrolls of the ancient Egyptians. They record the widespread use of garlic for its health-giving properties, especially for the slaves building the pyramids. Herbs were used in abun-

The herbs chamomile, lavender and evening primrose combine informally with the bright orange flowers of *Coreopsis* to form a tapestry of colour in the garden.

dance in the mummification of the dead, and rare herbs and spices were placed with the dead in their tombs.

Greek philosophers and physicians made extensive records of the uses and properties of herbs. Aristotle and Hippocrates recorded the value and cultivation of hundreds of herbs. But it was the Greek *Herbal of Dioscorides* compiled in the first century AD which for 1500 years became the source book for all herbalists. Dioscorides was a doctor in the Roman army during the reign of Nero and his five books provided details on more than 600 plants and their medicinal properties. This knowledge formed the basis of much of the research and learning of other great physicians and botanists who followed centuries later.

The Roman armies did much to promote and spread the use of herbs. Herbs were an integral part of the soldiers' diet and also provided the medicines to treat their wounds. As the Roman empire expanded, so did the knowledge of herbs. For the soldier on the march, the addition of herbs to salted and dried meat made them more palatable. As the Romans conquered ever farther afield, they themselves were introduced to new herbs by those they had subjugated. Rich herbal sauces thus became a staple part of the Roman diet.

The Roman Pliny (AD 23–79) created even more extensive early records on medicinal herbs, eight volumes in all, and such writings had a great influence on the esteemed English physician and astrologer Nicholas Culpeper, whose herbal published in 1653 is still treasured today as a reference. At the time Pliny was compiling his studies, scholars in Asia and India were also recording valuable information on the properties of herbs found in those regions.

Much later, the 16th century voyages of settlers and migrants to the New World, mainly to New England and Virginia, saw Europeans introduce many herbs they had cultivated for centuries and, in turn, the previously unknown herbs of the Americas flowed back to Europe.

For many centuries in Britain and Europe, sophisticated cultivation of herbs was left to religious orders in monasteries while peasants gathered wild herbs from the woods.

As Europe emerged from the Middle Ages witchcraft became very popular and many of the herbs used were potent drugs, some poisonous and hallucinogenic. Mandrake, deadly nightshade, hemlock and henbane were widely used. Concoctions of these plants were often smeared on the body and absorbed through the skin, inducing trances. It is from this period that many superstitions about herbs stemmed and some persist to this day. Rosemary, hyssop and angelica, for example, were for many centuries considered a valuable protection against evil.

Creeping rosemary was an important herb for warding off evil in medieval times.

By the 18th and 19th centuries herb gardens were a common and traditional sight in Europe, the herbs being used not only as a flavouring in cooking but also as preservatives.

As a flavouring, herbs were frequently used in sauces to disguise the odour of meats which were difficult to preserve and keep edible. In addition, herbs were used in making wine and beer, in perfumes and candles as well as in healing potions. Horehound tea was used in curbing coughs, lemon balm for a relaxing tea to soothe the nerves, sage was greatly valued, and still is, as a tonic, and comfrey was popular for staunching the wounds of battle.

With the advances of modern medicine the use of herbs for medicinal purposes faded rapidly in the Western world. Today's multicoloured, cellulose-coated pills are not only far more convenient for treating ailments than an array of herbs, but generally quicker acting and more effective. Scientists can reproduce the chemicals found in plants in more accurate, reliable and effective doses.

The ingredients in a particular plant can vary from day to day, season to season, according to conditions. A plant which could provide a cure for an ailment, at another time, using the same quantity, could provide a lethal overdose. Modern medicine can take the desired property, package it in a neat pill and eliminate that risk. On the other hand, the side effects of concentrated chemicals can also be harmful as they rush to other parts of the body not being treated — the brain, liver etc. — sometimes causing dizziness and nausea.

But for all the wonder of today's synthetic substitutes, the dependence on nature is still strong and there has been a world-wide resurgence of interest in the use of herbal remedies. Pharmaceutical companies spend millions of dollars every year on plant research and development in the hope of making discoveries to equal those of quinine and morphine.

The advent of refrigeration to a large degree spelled the end of the traditional home herb garden for a long time. There was no longer a need for herbs as a preservative and refrigerated, processed foods contained artificial flavourings. But with today's greater awareness of protecting the environment and the focus on healthy lifestyles and fitness, herbs have made a comeback not only in home cooking but also among the health-conscious who prefer nature to do its work rather than synthetic imitations.

While many people are now re-discovering the flavours and scents and calm to be found in a herb garden, even those living in apart-ments are able to develop mini herb gardens in pots and containers indoors. In the mod-ern high-powered, high-density living, the growing of herbs at home is building bridges back to nature and history.

Comfrey, also known as boneset, was tradition-ally used to treat the wounds of war.

Chapter 2

HERBS IN GARDEN DESIGN

A formal herb garden design.

NO other plants appear to offer such scope for innovative designs and themes as herbs. Herb garden designs can be plucked from the dim recesses of time and still be as attractive and intriguing as when first developed. Or the theme can be quite new, something that has evolved from modern living trends and pressures. The beauty of herbs is that their uses and attractions are timeless.

Herb garden themes can range from medicinal, religious, Oriental, scented and herbs for use as dyes to designs such as knotted gardens, Shakespearean gardens, container gardens, hanging gardens, herb lawns, miniature herbs and cottage herb gardens.

Central to the success of any theme or design is the careful plotting and selection of

This formal enclosed garden shows the effective colour combinations that can be achieved using herbs.

the correct plants for the location, whether it be sunny or shaded, cool or warm, sheltered or exposed, and the diligent preparation of the soil.

Take time to study the ultimate size and growth habits of the herbs chosen so that they can be correctly sited with tallest at the back down to ground huggers in the front.

Knot gardens

While many people today do not have the spacious gardens of old, this design is one that lends itself to adaptation for smaller, modern properties. The traditional Renaissance knot garden is an arrangement of low hedges which have been tightly trimmed to look like interwoven ribbons. Obviously the design can be more greatly appreciated if viewed from above, as was usually the case from the grand homes of this period.

The knot garden has an intriguing history.

It comes from the Middle Ages and was usually grown within castle walls. It was kept low and with flat tops, and predominantly consisted of lavender, box and rosemary. The flat tops allowed laundry to be spread over them to dry and in the process the clothes absorbed the scent of the herbs. Knot gardens were popular with Elizabethans for more than 100 years and gardeners skilled in developing them were well rewarded.

The over-and-under basket weave effect of knot gardens is achieved by the way the hedges are planted and pruned. A row of lavender would be planted, for example, and then a row of box would be planted close on either side at right angles, thus appearing to have disappeared underneath the lavender.

Plants need to be chosen for their ability to sustain heavy clipping, their low growing and dense habit and for their contrasting colours, to emphasise the individual ribbons.

Traditionally, knot gardens were square and symmetrical and bordered with boards, bricks or tiles. The soil between the hedges was either neatly raked or covered with different coloured gravel, ground lime, chalk dust or yellow clay. Today, bark is popular for these gardens or a range of scorias and pebbles. These are called open knots. Closed knot gardens are solidly filled with flowers instead.

Suitable plants for your 'ribbons' include dwarf English box, upright rosemary, lavender, grey santolina, thyme, hyssop, dwarf juniper and yew.

The knot garden is an intriguing challenge to one's creativity, can bring great delight, and once well established requires only careful grooming.

Herbs in containers

The versatility of potted herbs makes them invaluable in almost any setting... on the window-sill inside, on the patio or placed strategically as a feature in a larger landscape. They allow us to have a large garden in a very small place, gardens that can spill on to balconies and down steps. And because they are movable, they can be readily shifted about to either follow the sun or keep in the shade. The right potting mix will ensure that plants produce their best.

The choice of containers is almost limitless and this also allows one to express individuality. Containers can range from the traditional terracotta pots to stone or cast iron planters, baskets, clay and ceramic pots, barrels, tile drainpipes and wooden planter boxes. They can be placed individually or in complementary groupings.

It is important to choose a container suited to the size of the plant. If the plant is in a container that is too small it will dry out very

Five seasons herb growing in a terracotta pipe.

Sweet violets make a good underplanting for larger plants in containers. Here they combine with ferns beneath a fruit salad plant.

quickly, and should you forget to water regularly the plant will soon be lost. Transplant into increasingly larger containers as the plant grows. The final container should be large enough to allow the roots to grow and have good air and water circulation.

When re-using containers it is important to make sure they are clean, to avoid spreading disease from one plant to another. This is easiest done by scrubbing them out with a mixture of equal parts water and vinegar and giving them a final rinse with water containing a small amount of bleach.

In hot areas the use of non-porous containers, such as plastic and ceramic, helps to prevent plants drying out. If you are using porous containers such as untreated wood, terracotta and concrete, make sure they have

been soaked in water before use otherwise they will drag moisture from the potting mix when the herbs are first planted.

Just as important as the containers is the choice of plants that go in them. Culinary herbs such as sweet basil, chives, parsley, mints, tarragon and sage are always useful, but you might like to experiment with developing ethnic cuisine themes, such as Asian, Italian or French.

Mints are excellent for containers, not only for their scents and culinary uses, but the container prevents them from becoming rampant, as they so easily can in the wider garden. Apple mint, spearmint and bergamot, a member of the mint family Labiatae, are but a few mints that thrive in pots.

Experiment, too, with grouping your herbs. Try different herbs with the same flower colours, plants with variegated foliage or those with scented leaves. Some eye-catching combinations of shape and colour can be created. The brilliant green of curly parsley contrasts delightfully with the dark green of rosemary and the startling green of lime thyme looks great with variegated golden sage.

Groupings of different leaf shapes in the same large pot can look good, too. Try salad burnet, German chamomile and winter savory together, or sweet marjoram with thyme. It's a chance to experiment and a chance to show off your own creativity with the combinations you can put together.

Why not have a container collection featuring edible flowers? Chervil, violas, nasturtiums, dianthus and marigolds are a colourful and intriguing collection. The joy of container herb gardens is that you can have a wonderful time experimenting with colour, texture, form and foliage until you come up with just the right combination.

Above all, pay careful attention to the care and feeding of your plants and to the potting mix used. Container herbs are entirely dependent on you for their care, unlike plants in the garden. They need protection from extremes of weather, this can be done easily by moving them about, and regular feeding and watering.

Garden soil drains too slowly for use in containers, but garden centres have good supplies of potting mixes which drain quickly but retain nutrients and moisture long enough for the plants to take them up. Good drainage is the most important factor for container gardening.

Herbs in containers demand more frequent watering than if they were out in the garden because the soil in pots warms more quickly. But avoid placing saucers or trays under the pots except in very warm areas. Water contained by these will encourage root rot. If possible, it is a good idea, to place containers on bricks or plant stands to allow good air circulation.

Container plants also demand to be fertilised more often. Time release granules can be used and these should last for an entire season. Otherwise they need to be fed every 10 days or two weeks in the spring and summer. Their menu can include liquid seaweed fertiliser, fish emulsion or weak manure tea, among others.

Cared for regularly, plants in container gardens provide flexibility, fun and an endless opportunity to be creative.

Herbal lawns

Herbal lawns provide a delightful scented alternative to the traditional but sometimes bland sweep of lawn. But here is a case for thinking small rather than big. If you have visions of a large herbal lawn, be warned that they can not only be extremely costly but also hugely time-consuming to maintain.

A herbal lawn, however, can add a new perspective to that small space in the garden that might normally be a traditional lawn or it could be ideal for awkward strips between gardens. A traditional lawn could be maintained for most of the garden and a herbal lawn grown in a particular small area to add interest to an overall design.

Why a herbal lawn? When mown or walked upon they give off a pleasant fragrance, they can look attractive with some herbs having tiny flowers, and depending on the choice of herb, they can be used in a tea or even nibbled on.

There are three possibilities to consider: adding herbs to an existing lawn; starting a new lawn combining grass and herbs; or planting entirely in herbs, remembering we are considering only small areas.

The simplest method is adding herbs to an existing lawn. This can be done by cutting out 30 cm square patches at random spots of your choice, preferably in the late spring. It is a good opportunity to remove existing patches of lawn that are not looking particularly healthy. Fill the holes with good compost or topsoil and add your well-rooted seedlings.

The choice of herbs is extensive but some recommended ones include:

Chamomile, Roman (*Chamaemelum nobile*). One of the most popular plants for lawns, it has fine, bright green leaves radiating from a thick, central stalk and has little, daisy-like blossoms. When crushed underfoot, it releases an exciting aroma. The blossoms make a popular tea. Native to the Mediterranean.

Pennyroyal (*Mentha pulegium*). This has a strong, minty aroma and creeps along, rooting as it goes, and can self-seed. A perennial native to Europe, but not particularly hardy.

Thyme, creeping (*Thymus serpyllum*). Forms a low mat of small leaves that are nearly evergreen, with clusters of pinkish flowers in mid-summer. Leaves can be used for cooking and in a tea. Native to the Mediterranean.

Yarrow, common (*Achillea millefolium*). Finely divided, fernlike leaves remain fresh and green from early spring to late autumn. Has a pungent odour. Doesn't flower in a mowed lawn. Native to Europe.

If planted in the late spring, water the herbs each week throughout the summer as they get established. Mow lightly and carefully the first season.

Starting a new herbal lawn involves more work than adding to an existing lawn. Having gone through the normal preparations for planting a lawn, add about three herb seedlings of your choice per square metre, then oversow with grass seed. Keep moist and in about two weeks there should be a fuzz of grass showing along with the herbs.

If you are considering doing away with a lawn altogether and using only herbs, think small. On too large a scale, the cost of using herbs can be expensive, it can be difficult to

The non-flowering *Chamaemelum nobile* 'Treneague' makes a soft, fragrant lawn.

get started and maintenance takes a lot of work. On the other hand, it looks great.

Other themes

The theme of your herb garden is limited only by your imagination. Here are some other themes worth considering.

A medicinal tea garden

A wide range of common ailments can be treated with soothing teas from the herb garden and a medicinal herb garden provides a theme of great interest and practical application. A herbal tea, or infusion, is a quick and simple way of using fresh or dried herbs in remedies that can be drunk hot or cold. As a standard measure, two teaspoons of fresh herbs or one teaspoon of dried herbs is used for each cup of boiling water. Here are some common conditions and herbs which can provide relief.

Stress and tension: Chamomile tea is widely used to ease nervous tension and exhaus-

As the blues and mauves of catmint and *Ajuga* show, herbs can successfully combine with other plants to make a showy flowering display.

tion. Simply take a handful of chamomile flowers, or a teaspoon of dried chamomile, and a small sprig of lavender for each cup of boiling water. Strain and drink three times a day over several weeks. A teaspoon of dried chamomile flowers and two to three hop strobiles per cup of boiling water can be used to treat insomnia. Drink a cup just before bedtime but do not take with other sleep-inducing drugs.

Headaches: A tea using one sprig of rosemary and three leaves of betony per cup makes a relaxing tea to clear the head. Keep the pot covered to retain the oils. One or two cups a day is sufficient.

Hangover: So often we pay dearly for having a good time but our lady's milk thistle tea can provide a preventive. Put one teaspoon of milk thistle seed per cup of water in a pot and boil for ten minutes, then strain and drink while hot. Two or three cups of this during the day before going to a party can be a great help.

Travel sickness: Use a handful of peppermint leaves and a handful of chamomile flowers for a tea. Leave the tea to cool. Strain and put into a flask to take with you in the car and sip during the journey.

Cholesterol control: Southernwood tea, which has a strong flavour, can stimulate the liver and improve digestion. Use one sprig to one cup of water and drink before meals. This should not be used during pregnancy.

Flowering herbs

While many people perceive herbs as a collection of green and grey leaves, planting herbs for their colour rather than for their many other qualities can provide an attractive and very practical display. Look at using anise hyssop, calendula, marigold, chives,

Above: As a flowering herb, yarrow has few equals. It comes in a variety of brilliant colours, including the bright pink *Achillea* 'Cherry Pie'.
Below: Foxgloves, feverfew and sage combine with perennials in this colourful border planting.

sage, thyme, lavender and yarrow — just for a start.

Miniature herbs

For those who may have only a balcony or similar small space for a herb garden, miniature herbs may be the answer. It may be difficult to track down some of these plants but the effort will be rewarding.

Look for: the dwarf curry plant (*Helichrysum italicam* 'Nana'); 'Blue Boy' rosemary (*Rosmarinus officinalis*), a very compact prostrate plant with blue flowers and the bonus of culinary use; and the miniature version of lambs' ears (*Stachys candida*). This fascinating herb, with its tiny, woolly grey leaves and pale yellow flowers, grows only to 15 cm.

An Oriental flavour

A range of herbs favoured in Asian cooking can provide a tasteful theme. Among plants fitting into this category are garlic chives (*Allium tuberosum*), which also feature

Mexican marigold *Tagetes lucida*

attractive white flowers; the giant red mustard (*Brassica juncea crispifolia*); edible garland chrysanthemum (*Chrysanthemum coronarium*); coriander, also known as Chinese parsley, (*Coriandrum sativum*); and Vietnamese rau ram or Vietnamese mint (*Polygonum odoratum*) which is used as a souring herb in Asian cooking.

The fragrant garden

Stepping into a herb garden that overwhelms you with its fragrance and scent is truly one of the great experiences of gardening. This

Opposite: These gardens use herbs, along with other garden plants, to very different effect. The top picture provides a more formal setting to complement the paved pathway and low wall. The bottom picture has a wilder cottage-garden feel. But there is no doubt that both entice the visitor to see what is around the corner!

can be achieved quite simply by careful plant selection and planning. Some herbs naturally give off a strong aroma, while others need to be crushed in the hand or underfoot to bring out their fragrance, so bear this in mind when planting.

Among the most common and delightful of such plants are the scented pelargoniums, a native of South Africa. There are about 100 scented varieties giving off such fragrances as lemon, cinnamon, peppermint, rose and orange. By crushing a leaf, small beads of oil produced at the base of minute leaf hairs are released, thus emitting the fragrances.

Some of the most common of herbs are also among the most fragrant, including majorams, lavenders, rosemarys, lemon verbena, sages and fennel, and all are worth including in a fragrant theme garden.

Convenient culinary bed

A few square metres in a spot handy to the kitchen is all that is needed to provide sufficient herbs to add interest to day-to-day cooking. A wooden planter or other form of container sufficient to hold about 15 to 20 varieties is all that is required and is to be preferred to an in-ground plot. The planter is easier to maintain all year round, good quality potting soil can be used, ideal drainage assured and plants kept more manageable and more accessible.

Include in your bed the culinary basics such as parsley, chives, basil, garlic chives, thyme, rosemary, sage and fennel. In choosing other herbs, make sure they can be kept to a manageable size. Avoid any of the mints: they will simply over-run your planter and if you include ever popular oregano you will have to cut it back hard from time to time. The convenient culinary planter is not only practical but can also provide a fragrant and flowering display.

What herb where?

When designing your herb garden, be sure to place plants where they are most suited to grow. So often we allow our desires to come before those of the plants and because we like the idea of a certain plant in a certain place, we put it there regardless of the fact that it will not, be happy. While it might survive it most certainly will not display its best. There is nothing more satisfying than seeing a plant obviously thriving in its surroundings.

Apart from the joy it brings to see a healthy, happy plant, remember that a strong, well-grown specimen is much more capable of fighting off or recovering from attacks by pests or diseases.

The following lists will help you decide what to put where when designing the perfect herb garden.

Herbs for shady spots

Angelica	*Angelica archangelica*
Bergamot	*Monarda didyma*
Chervil	*Anthriscus cerefolium*
Foxglove	*Digitalis purpurea*
French sorrel	*Rumex scutatus*
Lady's mantle	*Alchemilla mollis*
Lemon balm	*Melissa officinalis*
Lovage	*Levisticum officinale*
Mint	*Mentha* spp.
Moneywort	*Lysimachia nummularia*
Parsley	*Petroselinum* spp.
Sweet cicely	*Myrrhis odorata*
Sweet woodruff	*Galium odoratum*

Herbs for hedges — 1–1.5 m

Lavender	*Lavandula dentata*
Rosemary, upright	*Rosmarinus officinalis*
Southernwood	*Artemisia abrotanum*
Sweet bay	*Laurus nobilis* (can train to grow higher than 1.5 m)

Herbs for hedges — up to 1 m

Lavender	*Lavandula viridis* (green flowered), *L.* 'Marshwood', *L. pendunculata*
Pelargonium	*Pelargonium* spp.
Tree wormwood	*Artemisia arborescens*
Rose	*Rosa* spp.

Herbs for walls

Creeping rosemary	*Rosmarinus officinalis* 'Prostratus'
Creeping thyme	*Thymus serpyllum*
Lavender	*Lavandula stoechas*

Herbs for paths, paving stones or seats

Roman chamomile	*Chamaemelum nobile* 'Treneague'
Thyme	*Thymus herba-barona, T. serpyllum*
Pennyroyal	*Mentha pulegium*
Sweet woodruff	*Galium odoratum* (needs shade)

Herbs with grey leaves

Catmint	*Nepeta mussinii*
Catnip	*Nepeta cataria*
Cotton lavender	*Santolina* spp.
Horehound	*Marrubium vulgare*
Lambs' ears	*Stachys byzantina*
Lavender	*Lavandula* spp.
Sea holly	*Eryngium maritimum*
Thyme	*Thymus fragrantissimus*
Wormwood	*Artemisia absinthium*

Herbs that spread

Bergamot	*Monarda didyma*
Mint	*Mentha* spp.
Pineapple sage	*Salvia rutilans*
Roman chamomile	*Chamaemelum nobile*
Soapwort	*Saponaria officinalis*
Tansy	*Tanacetum vulgare*
Thyme	*Thymus serpyllum, T. pulegioides, T. herba-barona*
Yarrow	*Achillea millefolium*

Herbs, deciduous

Elder	*Sambucus nigra*
Hyssop	*Hyssopus officinalis*
Lemon verbena	*Aloysia triphylla*
Southernwood	*Artemesia abrotanum*

Herbs, perennial, that die down in winter

Chives	*Allium schoenoprasum, A. tuberosum*
Costmary	*Chrysanthemum balsamita*
Comfrey	*Symphytum officinale*
Elecampane	*Inula helenium*
Horseradish	*Cochlearia armoracia*
Sweet cicely	*Myrrhis odorata*
Tarragon	*Artemisia dracunculus*
Valerian	*Valeriana officinalis*

Herbs with edible flowers

Bergamot	*Monarda didyma*
Borage	*Borago officinalis*
Marigold	*Calendula officinalis*
Elder	*Sambucus nigra*
Nasturtium	*Tropaeolum majus*
Pineapple sage	*Salvia rutilans*
Rose	*Rosa* spp.
Violet	*Viola odorata*

Herbs for dried arrangements

Sweet bay	*Laurus nobilis*
Clary sages	*Salvia horminum, S. sclarea*
Cornflowers	*Centaurea cyanus*
Cotton lavender	*Santolina* spp.
Lavenders	*Lavandula* spp.
Marjoram	*Origanum* spp.
Sea holly	*Eryngium maritimum*
Tansy	*Tanacetum vulgare*
Thymes	*Thymus* spp.
Wormwood	*Artemisia absinthium*
Yarrow	*Achillea millefolium*

Chapter 3

HERB CARE

Lambs' ears (foreground) and lady's mantle both
require excellent drainage.

HERBS are great to grow as their needs are easy to meet; so easy in some cases that they are considered weeds and wildlings. But if real success is to be had in the home herb garden then it's worth taking the trouble to research the needs, growth habits and conditions preferred by the herbs you choose. Not only are the results more satisfying, but the more you know of the herbs you grow, the more you will enjoy growing and using them.

This chapter provides a brief overview of the general needs of herbs. More specific information is provided within the list of herbs (Chapter 4).

Water

It is safe to say that most herbs prefer a sunny, dryish site. Too much moisture is a

Opposite: Foxgloves (*Digitalis purpurea*), like many herbs, require little care to grow well.

major cause of herb losses. Yet if your garden happens to be a damp one, don't despair: there are a number of herbs that thrive in those conditions, such as comfrey, mints, elecampane, sweet cicely or marshmallow, to name a few.

Herbs grown in well-drained soil are best watered in the early morning or late afternoon before the sun sets, leaving time for the foliage to dry before evening falls. Prolonged wet foliage in warm conditions encourages mould.

Grey-leaved plants or those with furry foliage tolerate dry spells well, but most others require a constant supply of moisture. This can be difficult in the height of summer so remember to mulch the herb garden in late spring. I use a good covering of organic compost which serves to slow evaporation while, at the same time, feeding the soil. But any permeable covering is suitable if applied

over a dressing of blood and bone — chipped bark, hay, grass clippings (not too thick), untreated sawdust or pebbles.

Container grown herbs need special attention to watering. In the heat of summer most pots should be watered twice a day and hanging gardens might even need more than this.

Shade

Sunny sites suit most herbs but there are those that prefer dappled, damp conditions; mints, lady's mantle, French sorrel, primroses, foxgloves, valerian, bergamot, chervil, sweet woodruff, lovage, lemon balm and angelica, for instance. Growing parsley in shade will delay flowering, making the leaves useable over a longer period.

Pruning

Maintenance of shape and vigour by pruning is an essential part of successful herb gardening. Constant clipping carried out in a

Although herbs generally require little care, with the right feeding and watering they can produce a wonderful display. Shown here are Nepeta, Achillea and Salvia.

culinary garden is not necessarily enough to promote good growth so seasonal pruning is needed. This involves ruthlessly cutting back herbs that become straggly and unattractive to encourage new, fresh, compact growth.

A general rule of thumb for pruning is to regularly snip off the spent flowers to encourage new buds to open, trim all over after flowering and cut the whole plant back by at least one third in the late autumn. Pruning of frost tender plants might better be left until late spring when all danger of frost is past

Feeding

Many hardy herbs will grow in stony, poor soils, but helping them along with judicious feeding results in much better plants. If you use too much chemical fertiliser you will get

A vital time to feed and water well is when your herb garden has been newly planted. Shown here are marigolds, foxgloves, anise hyssop, lambs' ears, salad burnet and catmint, and at the back golden elder and pineapple sage.

soft, lush, tasteless growth that is prone to insect attack. To be on the safe side it is best to use liquid fish or seaweed fertilisers, compost, blood and bone (sparingly) or make your own liquid fertilisers from the very herbs you grow. Comfrey is wonderfully nutritious and an armful of comfrey leaves makes a powerful liquid fertiliser if infused in a barrel of rainwater for about one month. The resulting foul-smelling liquid can be diluted 50/50 and safely used to feed the whole herb garden. Comfrey leaves also make a good natural mulch if simply laid under and around individual plants, and as they decompose they nourish the soil.

Just two applications of fertiliser per growing season is all that is needed in gardens with average soil to keep plants growing well — one in the late spring and one in mid-summer. Remember always to water the garden well before fertilising to avoid burning the roots through reverse osmosis.

Give a herb garden a dusting of lime every second year in the early spring.

Pests and diseases

In general, herbs are not greatly bothered by pests and diseases and even less so if they are growing in the right place in well maintained soil. And staying away from poisonous chemical sprays ensures the presence of beneficial insects in the garden which keep pest damage to a minimum.

Tolerance is also a factor. Be prepared to share a little of your herbs with insects.

When your plants become familiar to you it is easy to spot trouble, which can then be dealt with in the early stages before real damage is done.

Aphids

Many herbs belong to the botanical family

27

Umbelliferae, the flowerheads of which play host to beneficial insects like hoverflies that devour aphids. Along with ladybirds these 'friends' happily go about their business of keeping pest damage in check as long as no poisonous chemical sprays are used. A good jet of water from a hose also does much to dislodge aphids, as does a soapy spray made from an infusion of garlic, elder or basil.

Leaf miner
This pest is easy to see. It eats winding tunnels in the leaves of lovage and sorrel. Simply pick off the affected leaf and destroy.

Cabbage white butterfly
The caterpillars can quickly reduce the leaves of herbal members of the cabbage family like horseradish and rocket to a skeleton. Physical intervention is the answer — hand pick them off, usually from the back of the leaf, and destroy.

Scale
Scale can be seen on the leaves of bay trees as tiny brown waxy lumps clustered close to leaf veins. The leaves then become sticky and covered with sooty mould. Pruning takes care of the problem, or if noticed early enough simply rub the scale off with finger and thumb.

Slugs and snails
Keeping the garden free of debris and weeds greatly reduces the likelihood of slug and snail infestation. Avoid using chemical snail and slug bait which harms the birds that eat the snails. Dried sage or untreated sawdust sprinkled around seedlings acts as a good deterrent. Or you can trap them by slightly sinking a saucer of beer in the soil.

Rust
This fungal disease particularly affects mint. The first step is to cut off and destroy diseased leaves. To prevent reinfestation of new shoots in the spring from spores that drop off onto the soil surface, mulch the mint patch with straw in the autumn and burn it off.

Mildew
Spray affected plants with an infusion of sage or elder leaves.

Alternatives to manual and herbal pest control measures are commercial preparations of 'organic' pesticides. They come from 'natural' sources which do not harm the environment or beneficial insect populations. Most garden centres carry a full range of these products.

Propagation
Sowing seed
Sowing seed is the best method of propagating herb plants if a good number are needed. Even if you end up with many more seedlings than you want, it is a pleasure to be able to give some away.

Growing your own seedlings also allows you to choose the biggest and strongest specimen to grow on, thereby increasing your chances of a successful crop.

Sowing seeds early in spring under shelter, such as in a glasshouse or conservatory, means sturdy seedlings can be transplanted out into the garden as soon as the danger of frost is past. This gives them a head start, which means fresh herbs are ready for use early in the season.

Each year I sow seeds of sweet, bush and purple basil in plastic seed trays which are placed in the conservatory where it is warm and sunny. Use a commercial seed-raising mix tamped down firmly in the tray. Scatter the seeds on top, cover with a dusting of mix, thoroughly water with a hand-held sprayer and finally cover with plastic film.

In no time at all the seeds germinate, whereupon remove the plastic film for oxygen to get in and keep the tray watered. Once the seedlings are big enough to han-

dle, thin them out to 5 cm apart and allow them to grow on.

When the second set of leaves appears on each seedling, gently transplant them into individual plastic pots filled with potting mix. I put them outside in a shady spot for about a week, after which I move them to a brighter situation, liquid feed and make sure they are kept well watered. At your leisure, you can then transplant them into the garden to grow to maturity. I group some of them in larger terracotta pots handy to the kitchen.

I use the same method for any number of herbs I want to get off to a good early start. Later on when the weather warms you can sow seed directly into the garden where they are to grow. This requires a little preparation in the form of thorough weeding, followed by raking and smoothing the site. Then follow the same method as if sowing indoors, except for the plastic covering.

More attention needs to be paid to watering outdoors to make sure the seedlings never dry out. Sometimes birds or cats can be a bother, but they can be discouraged with a covering of chicken wire.

Cuttings

Many perennial herbs grow very easily from cuttings, which can either be struck in water, pots of sandy soil or, in many cases, directly in the garden. I have very few, if any, failures with cuttings taken in the spring when growth is fresh and vigorous. It is a simple matter of cutting, at a downward angle, a 5–10 cm non-flowering tip just above a bud. Remove all but the top two or three leaves and insert it into the chosen medium.

I usually take two cuttings, especially if it is a plant that I am not too familiar with, putting one in water and the other in sand to

There are many cultivated varieties of lavenders, and more appear each year. You can successfully propagate them by taking cuttings in autumn.

Root division of clump-forming herbs, such as lambs' ears and catmint shown here, is a good way to build up plant numbers for a mass display.

observe which method works best. Hardy herbs that I know are not fussy get tucked into a little prepared spot directly in the garden. Sometimes I cover them over with a glass jam jar for protection. Look under the individual listing of herbs to see which ones grow well from cuttings.

Root division

Dividing and replanting clump-forming herbs is a successful way of increasing stock. Simply lift the entire clump with a garden fork, gently prize apart the mass of roots, making sure that each section has growing shoots, and replant. This is best done in the autumn so that the new plants have time to form a good network of roots before the following spring.

Layering

Layering is another very simple method of propagating certain herbs, such as caraway, thyme, horehound and winter savory. It involves slightly wounding a long stem on the underside and pegging it down into the soil. Kept in contact with moist soil, new roots will grow from the wound and when sufficiently strong the rooted end can be detached and replanted.

Chapter 4

THE HERBS

Aloe vera *Aloe vera*

The definition of a herb is not clear cut, but generally speaking herbs are soft-stemmed (herbaceous), fragrant plants. Some trees and shrubs, however, are also popularly known as herbs due to their fragrant leaves or flowers. Many herbs are invasive weeds and I have omitted some that in my view are not suited to the home garden, either because they are highly poisonous or too rampant in their growth habits.

ALOE VERA *Aloe vera*

Description: A succulent perennial that forms a rosette of long, fleshy, narrow leaves with spiny edges. The leaves are filled with a bitter gel and coloured light green with white flecks. Clusters of tubular orangy flowers are produced on single leafless stalks in summer.

Growing: Best in tropical or dry sub-tropical climates with long hot summers, it can be grown in temperate climates but usually does not flower. The plant is propagated from 'pups' that grow at the base of the parent plant. These can be removed and planted up in a porous or sandy soil, watered once and left in a shaded spot to root. This they do readily. *A. vera* needs protection from frost and grows best in a sunny, well drained site.

Uses: An ancient herb that is still used for a multitude of ailments. Recent research shows that it rapidly promotes healing of superficial wounds and burns, including radiation and sunburn. *A. vera* juice is taken as a general tonic and for relief of arthritis. The gel from the leaves is widely used in cosmetics such as face creams, shampoos and skin lotions.

ANGELICA *Angelica archangelica*

Description: A biennial with large, bright green, indented leaves similar to celery. The

Anise hyssop *Agastache foeniculum*

spring of the plant's second year. The whole plant dies after setting seed.

Uses: Stems are candied or can be cooked with rhubarb and other tart fruit to reduce tartness and sugar requirements. Dried or fresh leaves can be made into a tisane to aid digestion, coughs and colds. Seeds and seed oil flavour desserts and liqueurs, particularly chartreuse.

ANISE *Pimpinella anisum*

Description: A sprawling annual from the Mediterranean which needs at least 120 frost-free days to ripen seeds. The first leaves are tiny and strap-like, then they develop into larger, coarsely toothed leaflets and lastly, become small and ferny. If supported it can reach 50 cm high. Tiny white or yellow flowers are produced in 1 cm lacy umbels in mid-summer followed by the grooved, grey seeds that hang from thin stems in pairs.

Growing: Fresh seed sown in early spring, either indoors or out depending on the climate, can take as long as 28 days to germinate. Anise will grow in poor, dry soil in full sun but should be sheltered from wind as the plant easily blows over.

Uses: An ancient herb whose leaves and seeds are widely used in drinks, flavourings and salads. Liqueurs containing aniseed include anisette, pernod, sambuca and ouzo. Tea made from dried leaves or seeds aids digestion and eases coughs and colds.

ANISE HYSSOP
Agastache foeniculum

Description: Anise hyssop is a striking herbaceous perennial that grows more than 1 m high when in full flower. In summer, it produces 12–20 cm tall conical spires of tiny, lavender flowers, full of nectar and very attractive to bees. The stalked leaves are deep green with a tinge of purple and heart-shaped with serrated edges. The whole plant has a strong anise scent.

first-year plant sends down a sturdy root from which grow a clump of stemless leaves. The following summer, a thick, hollow, ribbed flower stem shoots up bearing leaves and 25 cm umbels of small, greenish-white flowers. Bees, flies and wasps love them. From the flowers come ribbed green seeds which turn light brown when ripe. A mature plant can reach 2 m high.

Growing: Angelica grows best in dappled shade with deep, rich, moist soil. Sow fresh, ripened seed mid to late summer or early spring when germination takes 3 to 4 weeks at 16–20 °C. Seeds need light to germinate so just press them into prepared soil and keep well watered. Thin seedlings to 1 cm apart to allow adequate growing space. Leaves and stems are best harvested when tender, in the

Growing: This plant self-sows quite readily in the right situation or can be grown from seed sown in spring or autumn. It prefers, and flowers best, in a sunny location, away from wind, in average, well drained soil.

Uses: Dried or fresh, the leaves make a delightful anise flavoured herb tea. Dried flowers and leaves hold their fragrance well so make good additions to pot-pourri. The dried flower spikes also look wonderful, sprayed gold, in festive floral arrangements.

ARNICA *Arnica montana*

Description: Arnica is a poisonous perennial herb that first forms a basal rosette, then opposite, hairy stemmed leaves. The sunflower-like, deep yellow flowers are produced terminally and from the leaf nodes on erect stems 10–60 cm tall.

Growing: Arnica comes from European mountain areas so needs cool moist conditions to grow well. It can be propagated by root division or grown from seeds sown in early spring.

Uses: Arnica is a medicinal herb that is well known as an aid for healing sprains and bruises. It is applied externally only in the form of liniments or salves. When applied to the scalp it is believed to promote hair growth.

Bush basil *Ocimum basilicum minimum*

BASIL *Ocimum* spp.

Description: The annual basils are ancient herbs with a recorded history that goes back to the first century AD. A number of different varieties are grown but the most popular are bush basil (*O. basilicum minimum*), sweet basil (*O. basilicum*) and purple basil (*O. basilicum purpurascens*). All types have a strong clove-like fragrance.

Bush basil *O. minimum* Bush basil grows into a compact, rounded mound of small, shiny green leaves. The flavour is more bitter than that of sweet basil. Spikes of white flowers are thrown up in summer.

Sweet basil *O. basilicum* Sweet basil grows to about 50 cm high, with branching stems and 3–5 cm long, ovate, shiny leaves. The flowering spikes are greenish white. The whole plant is strongly fragrant. This is the most commonly used culinary flavouring herb.

Basil *Ocimum basilicum* 'Green Ruffles'

Above: Sweet basil *Ocimum basilicum*
Below: Bear's breeches *Acanthus mollis*

Purple basil *O. basilicum purpurascens*
Purple basil has the same growth habit as sweet basil but the flower spikes are pale pink and the leaves dark purple.

Growing: Basils grow easily from seed sown in a warm, sunny situation in spring once all danger of frost has passed. They thrive in rich, composty soil with plenty of moisture. To promote bushiness and prevent flowering, nip the tips of shoots.

Uses: For centuries, sweet basil tea made from the leaves has been prescribed for nausea, gas and dysentery. Basils are one of the most popular culinary herbs in Italian cuisine, where their combination with tomatoes is legendary.

BEAR'S BREECHES *Acanthus mollis*

Description: *Acanthus mollis* is a striking perennial thistle with beautiful, large, glossy, prickly, deeply-cut leaves and tall, stately, purple and white flower spikes. When in flower, the plant stands more than 1 m and has an equal spread.

Growing: *A. mollis* likes full sun but will grow in semi-shaded positions, where it produces fewer flowers. A well-drained, deep loam or sandy soil is best. The plant is propagated by division in autumn or spring-sown seed, that germinates readily.

Uses: Nowadays, *Acanthus* is grown mostly as a decorative plant and for use in dried flower arrangements. In the past it was used as a medicinal herb to relieve gout, scalds and burns.

BERGAMOT *Monarda didyma*

Description: Bergamot is a beautiful perennial herb with mid-green, 10–15 cm hairy leaves that grow opposite each other from upright, square stems. It spreads by runners. Brilliant red, spider-like fragrant flowers are produced mid to late summer on tall stems that can reach up to 1 m in height.

Growing: Bergamot needs rich, moist soil

Bergamot *Monarda didyma*

in a full sun or semi-shaded position. Propagation is by division in early spring. Old clumps should be lifted, dead roots removed and new runners re-planted.

Uses: The dried leaves and flowers are used in tea and pot-pourri. In the United States it is known as Oswega tea, as it was enjoyed by the Oswega Indians who first introduced it to early settlers. Medicinally it is said to promote sleep when added to boiling milk.

BETONY *Stachys officinalis*

Description: Betony is a perennial matt-forming plant with pretty, deep green, oblong leaves with serrated edges. Flowering stems up to 50 cm tall appear in summer carrying spikes of dark pink/lilac flowers. A large flowered form *S. o.* 'Grandiflora' is available.

Growing: Betony is a hardy plant that is easily grown in sun or semi shade. Average soil with plenty of organic matter and good drainage will suit it well. Propagation is by division or seed in spring.

Uses: Betony was once a highly respected and sought after herb used medicinally to treat many illnesses, especially tension headaches and melancholy. Today, a tea made from the leaves of betony is prescribed to treat depression and dull headaches. The flowers can be dried for floral arrangements.

BORAGE *Borago officinalis*

Description: Borage is a prickly, upright annual with large, oval leaves growing alternately from hollow stems. It grows from 1–3 m in height. Small, dainty, radiant blue, star-shaped flowers with prominent black stamens are produced from early spring to late autumn.

Growing: Borage will grow almost anywhere but does best in full sun and friable soil. It is grown from seed sown in autumn or spring and self-seeds profusely.

Uses: Young leaves, finely chopped, and flowers can be used in salads. They have a flavour similar to cucumber. The individual flowers can be frozen in ice cubes and added to drinks or candied and eaten as a sweet.

Borage *Borago officinalis*

Caraway *Carum carvi*

Catmint *Nepeta mussinii*

CARAWAY *Carum carvi*

Description: Caraway is a biennial herb that grows to 60 cm high with feathery, carrot-like foliage. In the summer of the second year it produces umbels of white flowers followed by the familiar caraway seeds.

Growing: Caraway is grown from seed or allowed to self-sow, which it will do freely. It is not fussy about soil, thrives in full sun but resents moist conditions. Spring-sown seeds require two seasons to produce a crop whereas autumn-sown seeds will render a crop the following summer.

Uses: Medicinally and as a spice, caraway has been used since the Stone Age. Caraway seeds are valuable as a flavouring for savoury foods, breads, cakes and are a well-known aid to digestion. Young leaves can be chopped and added to salads or soups, the roots boiled and eaten as a vegetable, and a tisane from the seeds is mild enough to give to children for digestive or bowel com-plaints. Chewing the seeds also sweetens the breath.

CATMINT
Nepeta mussinii, N. x faassenii

Description: Catmint is a most attractive perennial herb with grey-green, heart shaped, toothed leaves and terminal spikes of tiny lilac or white ('snowflake') flowers. It grows to 20 cm high and forms a rounded clump. A popular taller cultivar is 'Six Hills Giant'.

Growing: Catmint prefers limey soil, adequate drainage and full sun, but will also grow satisfactorily in dappled shade and average soil. Propagation is by root division in early spring or autumn in warmer regions.

Uses: Cats love catmint which is a good reason to include it in the herb garden. Young plants need protection though or cats will crush and flatten them. The flowers are also very attractive to bees.

CATNIP *Nepeta cataria*

Description: Catnip is also erroneously known as catmint and while it belongs to the same family it is, in fact, a larger plant all round reaching almost 1 m in height. The leaves are similar but bigger and have a minty fragrance, while the flowers are white tinged pink with purple spots and appear at the ends of the main stem and branches.

Growing: Catnip self-sows freely if flowering stems are not cut back as flowers fade. It is easily grown from seed or root division in the autumn or spring. Average garden soil in a sunny situation suits it well. Allow for the spreading stems of catnip by planting at least 50 cm apart.

Uses: Catnip tea has long been used to relieve gas pains and chewing the fresh leaves is said to give relief from toothache. Like catmint, cats love this plant, both to roll in and eat.

CHAMOMILE

Roman chamomile, *Chamaemelum nobile*; **German chamomile**, *Matricaria recutita*

Description: There are two types of chamomile available — one is an annual and commonly known as German, true or wild chamomile (*Matricaria recutita*). This is the one used medicinally. The other is a perennial commonly known as Roman or lawn chamomile whose chief use is as a carpeting herb. The variety 'Treneague' is most popular for lawns as it is non-flowering and tightly ground hugging. Both types are low growing with soft ferny foliage and white daisy-like flowers with yellow centres. German chamomile has single ray florets and Roman, double. When crushed, chamomiles release a fresh apple fragrance.

Growing: Both types grow readily from seed sown in the autumn or early spring. Lawn chamomile can also be grown from

Catmint *Nepeta mussinii* 'Six Hills Giant'

German chamomile *Matricaria recutita*

rooted suckers. Average garden soil is suitable, provided it is well weeded and finely raked. Full sun and good drainage are essential for real success.

Uses: Roman chamomile is mainly used as a fragrant lawn. German chamomile has been valued in Europe for centuries for the healing oil extracted from the fresh flowers. Small amounts are used to treat a wide range of ailments, such as stomach pains due to nervous upset, toothache, cystitis and rheumatism. Skin problems including eczema, boils and abscesses are treated with infusions and compresses. Chamomile tea made by infusing flowers for 3–5 minutes in boiling water is legendary as a soothing drink. Chamomile flowers can also be used as a hair rinse both to nourish and lighten fair hair.

CHERVIL *Anthriscus cerefolium*

Description: Chervil is an aromatic annual that resembles parsley but is generally taller (50 cm) and the leaves are paler, more finely cut and lacy looking. The flowers are white and grow in tiny umbels. The delicate flavour combines well with tarragon, parsley and chives to make up the well-known 'fines herbes' of French cuisine.

Growing: Chervil is a cool weather plant and should be sown in the early spring or late autumn for a spring crop. Growing it in the heat of summer burns the delicate leaves which turn pink. It grows well in medium to light soils with plenty of compost. The leaves are ready for harvest approximately 6–8 weeks after sowing.

Uses: Chervil can be used generously to enhance the flavour of soups and sauces. The French use it more liberally than parsley both as a garnish and as an addition to salads. Medicinally it has been used as a poultice on aching joints.

The flowers of chervil *Anthriscus cerefolium*.

CHICORY *Cichorium intybus*

Description: Looks much like a dandelion with a rosette of toothed basal leaves but unlike dandelion the flower stalk, bearing smaller leaves, can grow up to 100 cm and branch several times. In mid-summer stalkless, radiant blue, 3 cm wide flower heads form singly or in twos or threes in the axils of the stem leaves. The flowers open early in the morning and close five hours later. Many varieties of chicory are available with variations in leaf size and appearance, e.g., witloof, looseleaved, curly leaved and red-green.

Growing: Chicory is grown from seed sown in early spring, or where winters are mild in late autumn for spring harvest. Well prepared, rich garden soil suits best but it will grow in a wide variety of soils in a sunny position. Mature clumps can be divided in autumn and reset.

Uses: The blanched leaves of some varieties are used in salads, or cooked as a green vegetable. Young roots can be boiled and eaten like parsnips or dried, roasted and added to coffee.

CHIVES *Allium schoenoprasum*

Description: Chives are well known, perennial, bulbous plants, which are members of the onion family. Their thin, round, hollow leaves grow in a fountain-like shape from clumps of small, white, flat bulbs. In summer, pretty pom-poms of pale purple flowers appear on stiff, erect stems. Garlic chives (*A. tuberosum*) have a stronger flavour with thin flattened leaves.

Growing: Chives are heavy feeders so should be grown in rich soil containing lots of organic fertiliser. They need full sun and plenty of moisture in dry spells. Propagation is usually by division of clumps in the spring or autumn or seed sown in the spring. Annual division and resetting of clumps is recommended to avoid death by overcrowding. Gently lift the entire clump, tease off six bulbs at a time and set them about 15 cm apart.

Uses: Chives give a delicate onion flavour to a wide range of cooked food. The leaves are usually chopped finely and sprinkled on the finished dish. They greatly enhance the flavour and appearance of scrambled eggs, mashed potatoes, cream and cottage cheeses and a variety of salads. A favourite garnish for vegetable soups is a dollop of sour cream sprinkled with chives. Like all onions, chives contain antibiotic properties and help the body to break down fatty foods.

CLARY SAGE

Annual clary, *Salvia horminum*;
biennial clary, *Salvia sclarea*

Description: Annual clary, *S. horminum*, is a thoroughly delightful form that is easily grown from seed, each one rising in a branching stem about 50 cm high and terminating in a spike of brightly coloured bracts, some purple, some pink and others whitish green. The leaves are typically sage-like, grey-green and rough to touch but small and rounded. The actual flowers are white and

Chives *Allium schoenoprasum*

insignificant in comparison to the brilliant bracts.

Biennial clary, *S. sclarea*, is a striking version that grows over 1 m in height with large 30 cm long, pebbly, heart shaped, hairy grey leaves. They are arranged in stalkless pairs on stiff, brownish, square stems. Flowers bloom in the second year in the form of

Clary sage, annual, *Salvia horminum*

spikes with pale blue or white flowers and larger pale pink bracts. Allow at least half a metre between plants and stake to prevent untidiness.

Growing: Clary sages are grown from seed that easily germinates and they readily self-sow. They thrive in alkaline soils that are light and well drained. Lightly fed and watered in dry weather, both varieties produce a stunning show.

Uses: Biennial clary enjoys a long history of medicinal use, one being as Culpeper describes to 'clear eye' of foreign objects, hence 'claru'. When soaked, the seeds produce a thick mucilage. This was placed in the eye to treat inflammation and displace any foreign matter. Culpeper recommended using the mucilage to draw out splinters or thorns from the flesh. The plant was also employed to treat indigestion and liver complaints. In France clary sage oil is used as a fixative in the perfume industry and the flowering tops were steeped in wine to produce a muscatel flavour.

Annual clary is useful only in dried arrangements and the brightly coloured bracts hold colour well when dried.

COMFREY *Symphytum officinale*

Description: Comfrey is a perennial with an erect, hairy stem from which grow alternate oval, dark green, hairy leaves. The lower leaves grow to 25 cm long and reduce in size up the stem. Small, bell-shaped flowers coloured purple, cream, pink or blue are produced in spring and summer and hang down in drooping clusters.

Growing: Propagation is by root division in the autumn or by seed. In fact, once comfrey is introduced into the garden you will have it for life because new plants grow from the smallest piece of root. In rich, damp situations comfrey will flourish in sun or semi-shade.

Uses: While once considered an extremely nutritious and medicinal vegetable, recent

Comfrey *Symphytum x uplandicum*

research has shown that comfrey may cause cancer if taken over a long period of time. In Australia, the use of comfrey as an internal medication is banned but still available as an ointment for healing surface sores and broken bones. Hence its common names 'knitbone' or 'boneset'.

CORIANDER *Coriandrum sativum*

Description: Before flowering, coriander somewhat resembles parsley but has paler green, more loosely formed, round leaves. It is an annual herb that grows to 50 cm in height and produces dainty umbels of pale pink flowers followed by bunches of small green berries that gradually turn beige and become ridged as they ripen. Before this stage, however, the whole plant has a strange smell bordering on unpleasant, but when the seeds are ripe it becomes sweetly aromatic.

Growing: Coriander grows easily from seeds sown in autumn in temperate climates or spring in cold temperatures. Full sun and soil that is light and fertile suits this herb best.

Coriander *Coriandrum sativum*

Costmary *Chrysanthemum balsamita*

Uses: Coriander is best known for its seeds which are widely used in Indian cookery. The leaves are often known as 'cilantro' and can be used to flavour soups and salads or as an attractive and more nutritious garnish than parsley. The ground seed is used in curry powder and various spice combinations used for flavouring sausages.

CORNFLOWER *Centaurea cyanus*

Description: Cornflower is an annual herb that in some countries grows wild, but it is also widely cultivated in gardens throughout the world. Brilliant blue, pink and white flowers grow from long, wiry, branching stems throughout the summer. The plant grows to half a metre and the flowers look almost suspended amid a sea of narrow, downy green leaves.

Growing: Cornflowers are easily grown from seed and will readily self-sow in the right conditions. Seeds sown in spring will produce lots of flowers over the whole summer. Provide reasonable soil, full sun or dappled shade.

Uses: The primary use of cornflowers is in dried arrangements and pot-pourris. The plant dries very well and the flowers hold their colour beautifully. In times gone by, a decoction of the flowers was used to treat inflamed eyes.

COSTMARY
Chrysanthemum balsamita
syn. *Tanacetum balsamita*

Description: Costmary is a perennial with a two-stage growth habit. It has a creeping rootstock from which grow 10–15 cm bright green, stalked, slightly toothed leaves with a strong mint fragrance. In the summer, 1 m high flowering stalks appear with much smaller leaves and yellow button-like flowers. The whole plant dies back in winter.

Growing: Propagation of costmary is by root division in spring, which needs to be done every few years to keep the plant healthy. Full sun and average garden soil suit well, together with sufficient space to develop a good clump.

Uses: The common names of costmary are 'alecost' and 'bibleleaf'. Alecost refers to its previous use in flavouring ale and bibleleaf from the custom of pressing a leaf to make a fragrant bookmark. The leaves are used in herbal tea or in small quantities to flavour certain foods. In the Middle Ages it was used as a medicinal powder to aid a range of ills.

COTTON LAVENDER *Santolina* spp.

Description: Ten species of cotton lavender are grown as hardy dwarf shrubs ranging in height from 20–60 cm. Commonly found in herb gardens is *S. chamaecyparissus* which grows to about 50 cm, forming a neat mound of silver-grey, fine-toothed leaves with small, round, yellow flowers. It is often used as low hedging as it can be constantly clipped.

Growing: Cotton lavenders like full sun and average garden soil that drains well. It is important to keep bushes well clipped or they tend to become straggly. After flowering, prune back hard to keep the bushy appearance. Propagation is by seed, layering or heel cuttings.

Uses: The leaves of cotton lavenders may be dried and used in mothbags to protect clothing. The flowers and leaves are valued for use in dried arrangements. Traditionally, the plants are used as low border hedging in the herb garden.

CURRY PLANT
Helichrysum angustifolium

Description: Curry plant is a sub shrub that forms an attractive mound of silver, needle-like leaves topped with dull, golden clusters of flowers produced in summer. It is a half-hardy perennial plant with a height that ranges from 15–30 cm and a width from 25–50 cm. The whole shrub smells strongly of curry. Also look for the dwarf curry plant *H. italicum* 'Nana'.

Growing: Like most grey-leaved plants, curry plant is drought tolerant. It requires full sun and light to sandy soil to grow well. Propagation is by seed or from tip cuttings taken in spring or woody cuttings taken in the autumn. Prune lightly after flowering to maintain a good shape.

Uses: The leaves can be chopped and added to mild foods to impart a barely discernible curry flavour. The plant smells a lot stronger than it tastes. The flowers dry well and are useful in dried arrangements. The dried leaves are used as a moth repellant.

DANDELION *Taraxacum officinale*

Description: Dandelion is a common garden weed, a perennial which grows wild all over the world. From a strong, fleshy tap root, a rosette of narrow toothed leaves forms the base from which 5–25 cm flowering stalks appear from early spring to late autumn. The bright yellow flowers comprise a mass of tiny florets, rich in nectar and most attractive to bees. These are followed by the familiar fluffy-balled seed head.

Growing: Cultivation of dandelion in good soil renders plants that are more edible than their wild counterparts. Propagate by seed or division of roots and if self-sowing is not required, remove flower heads before seed sets.

Uses: Dandelion is a wholesome food containing protein, fat, vitamins, and a range of mineral salts. The bitter flavour comes from the presence of glycosides and tannins. All parts of the plant can be eaten. The root is dried, roasted and ground to make dandelion coffee; the young leaves are added to salads or lightly cooked as a vegetable; and the flowers can be made into a light wine that is said to be good for the blood.

DILL *Anethum graveolens*

Description: Dill is a decorative, fragrant annual of the parsley family. It grows to 1 m in height, has bluey-green, feathery leaves, somewhat like fennel, and in summer produces rounded umbels of yellow flowers followed by small seeds. (One head produces an estimated 25,000 seeds.)

Growing: A wide range of soils is suitable for growing dill. Provide full sun or afternoon shade in very hot climates with plenty of water. Sow seeds at two weekly intervals from early spring to ensure a constant supply of leaves.

Uses: No fish dish is complete without dill leaf or dill weed as it is sometimes called. It also adds interest to soft cheeses, particularly feta, white meats, soups and stews. Dill seeds are used in pickles, breads, slaws and stuffings.

ECHINACEA *Echinacea purpurea*

Description: Echinacea is a hardy, herbaceous perennial with rough, narrow leaves and tall flowering stems of single, purple-crimson, daisy-like flowers. The petals hang back from a distinctive, raised, dark orange, conal centre. The plants are slow growing and can reach over 1 m in height.

Growing: Grow echinacea in fertile, well drained soil in a sunny position. Propagate by root division and replanting in autumn or sowing seed indoors in early spring. Prolong flowering by deadheading regularly.

Uses: Echinacea now outsells most other herbal remedies for colds and flu as it helps the body defend itself against viral infection. Cut flowers have a long vase life.

ELDER *Sambucus nigra*

Description: The elder is a very attractive, bushy deciduous shrub or small tree that grows up to 5 m in height. It has mid-green, pinnate leaves with jagged edged leaflets. In spring, creamy-coloured, flattened flowers in umbels 15 cm across are borne. These are followed by round, shiny black berries (in cool areas only). Popular varieties include *S. nigra* 'Aurea' which produces bright golden

Top: Cotton lavender *Santolina chamaecyparissus*
Middle: Curry plant *Helichrysum angustifolium*
Bottom: Echinacea *Echinacea purpurea*

young foliage and *S. nigra* 'Aurea Variegata' with yellow-margined leaves.

Growing: Elders can be grown from seed or hardwood cuttings taken in early spring. Moist soil, plenty of sunshine and hard winter pruning ensure plenty of flowers and good berry crops. Berries do not develop well in warm, humid climates.

Uses: The uses for all parts of the elder are many, ancient and legendary, but today the berries are mostly used to make elderberry wine and the flowers fried in batter to make fritters. Medicinally, the berries can be made into an ointment for burns, a salve for sore eyes and a cough mixture. Leaves and bark were used as purgatives and the whole shrub can be used as a dye.

ELECAMPANE *Inula helenium*

Description: Elecampane is a perennial herb that can reach 2 m tall when in flower. It has large, ovate, pointed leaves with serrated edges and bright yellow sunflower-like flowers borne on branched stems in the summer. The root smells strongly of violets.

Growing: Elecampane grows easily in sun or semi-shade in average garden soil and should be given enough space (about 1 m all around) to develop fully. It is propagated by division of roots in autumn or spring, or grown from seed sown in spring.

Uses: The use of elecampane as a medicinal herb dates back to the time of the ancient Greeks when it was used in the treatment of colds, asthma, coughs and stomach ulcers. Its common names, 'horseheal' and 'scabwort', refer to the veterinary use of the plant in curing skin eruptions on sheep and horses.

EVENING PRIMROSE
Oenothera biennis

Description: Evening primrose is a hardy biennial that has escaped cultivation in some countries and is considered a weed. It has

Evening primrose *Oenothera biennis*

long, narrow, pale green leaves which form a rosette in the first year, followed by up to a 2 m high stem carrying a profusion of delicate, dish-like, translucent yellow flowers early in the second year. The flowers open successively in the late afternoon and stay open until the next morning. They last for one or two nights only and are sweetly scented.

Growing: This plant will self-sow quite freely if allowed to go to seed. It can also be grown from seed sown in spring in light soil in full sun. Protection from wind is advisable as the stems are inclined to blow over.

Uses: All parts of this plant are edible, including its seeds, which look like poppy seeds. Young leaves can be eaten raw in salads and the sturdy nut-flavoured taproot can be boiled like parsnips. Native Americans used evening primrose in a variety of medicinal ways: as a poultice for bruises, as a tea to reduce weight, and as treatment for upset stomachs. Recent research has also proved evening primrose oil to be an important treatment for essential fatty acid deficiency.

FENNEL

Wild fennel; *Foeniculum vulgare*;
bronze fennel, *F. v.* 'Rubrum';
Florence fennel, *F. dulce*

Description: Wild fennel can be seen growing in wasteland and beside roads throughout the world. Tall, 2–3 m, feathery-leaved wands grow from a central base. In summer, flat umbels of tiny yellow flowers are produced, followed by the familiar small ribbed seeds. The whole plant has a strong aniseed fragrance. It is a perennial which dies down after flowering and dispersing seed.

Bronze fennel is a smaller plant (1–2 m) whose feathery foliage is a true bronze colour and the flowers a slightly darker shade of yellow.

Florence fennel grows to 2 m high, has blue-green fernlike foliage and succulent leaf bases that swell to form a bulb.

Growing: Grow fennel from seed and thin to 50 cm apart after germination. Average garden soil is suitable and an open, sunny situation is best. Fennel is drought-tolerant although Florence fennel benefits from good garden conditions and plenty of moisture during dry spells.

Uses: Fennel has been used for food and medicine for thousands of years in its native Mediterranean home. Seeds can be chewed to relieve hunger, aid digestion, sweeten breath and relieve flatulence. In the kitchen the leaves are used as a garnish, added to salads and other foods. Seeds enhance the flavour of cooked apple, bread, scones and muffins. Florence fennel can be added to casseroles and soups, or steamed and served with white sauce.

FENUGREEK
Trigonella foenum-graecum

Description: Fenugreek is a hardy, erect annual legume which grows to 50 cm high and resembles alfalfa in that the leaves comprise three distinct toothed leaflets. In summer, fragrant, creamy, stalkless flowers bloom followed by long, slender, hay-coloured pods containing around 16 seeds.

Growing: Like beans, fenugreek is easily grown from seed sown in late spring when all danger of frost is passed. This herb needs average soil and full sun and takes about four warm months to mature. Pick pods when they turn brown or pull up the entire plant and hang to dry.

Uses: Ground fenugreek seeds are one of the main ingredients in curry powder. In Indian cooking, the seeds are used with meat, potatoes and egg plant and the bitter leaves are cooked as a potherb. The seeds can be sprouted and used in salads and oil of fenugreek is used by the food industry as a maple flavouring. Since ancient times, the seeds have been used in tonics for horses and cattle, and to treat diabetes in humans.

FEVERFEW
Chrysanthemum parthenium

Description: Feverfew is a hardy but short-lived perennial with pale green, deeply

Feverfew *Chrysanthemum parthenium*.

Goat's rue *Galega officinalis*

divided leaves. It is bushy in appearance and grows up to 50 cm in height. It is often grown as an annual as it produces masses of white flowers in the first season. A popular variety, 'Aureum', has gold-green foliage with single white flowers.

Growing: Full sun, average soil and reasonable drainage suit this herb well. It can be grown from root division, seed or cuttings taken in spring. It also self-sows and is easily transplanted. Prune the bush well after flowering.

Uses: Trials carried out at the City of London Migraine Clinic in 1985 showed that feverfew is effective in reducing the symptoms of migraine headache when either the leaves are chewed or a tisane is drunk.

FIVE SEASONS HERB
Coleus amboinicus

Description: This herb is a sprawling plant with hairy stems and soft, fleshy, succulent-like leaves with serrated edges. The pale green leaves grow in opposite pairs from pinkish hairy stalks. Insignificant pale pink flowers are produced in terminal spikes in late summer. The whole plant has a strong oregano/thyme smell.

Growing: Five seasons herb is a tropical plant requiring warm, frost-free conditions to grow well. It needs very light, well-drained soil and full sun. I grow this herb in a warm sheltered spot in a series of terracotta drain pipes which are placed upright against a warm sunny wall. Here the herb enjoys warmth, perfect drainage and makes an attractive cascading feature. Propagation is usually by cuttings taken in spring and summer.

Uses: Having the flavour of oregano means that the finely-chopped leaves of five seasons herb combine well with Italian dishes, casseroles and soups.

FOXGLOVE *Digitalis purpurea*

Description: The magnificent spires of pink, apricot, white or purple tubular flowers produced by this herb belies its extremely poisonous nature. It is a biennial plant that in the first year produces a rosette of long, lance-shaped green leaves. The flowers bloom in the second year on tall (up to 150 cm) stems with diminishing sized alternate leaves.

Growing: Foxgloves grow wild in many areas of the world so can be easily cultivated in any average garden soil with reasonable drainage, preferably in dappled shade. Propagation is by seed sown in autumn or spring. It self-sows readily.

Uses: Foxgloves are grown commercially for use in the treatment of heart disease. The leaves contain the drug digoxin, a well known cardiac stimulant, and are usually harvested while the plant is in flower.

GARLIC *Allium sativum*

Description: This relative of the lily is a perennial, but usually grown as an annual, with long, flat, strap-like leaves that grow on an erect stem which orginates from a multi-cloved bulb. It grows to 60 cm high. In summer, small, clustered, pink and white flowers are borne on erect stems.

Growing: Garlic is easily grown from individual cloves taken from the outside of the bulb and set in light soil that has been enriched with organic fertiliser. In a sunny, warm situation it will grow well, providing it is kept well watered in dry times. It is said that garlic planted on the shortest day can be harvested on the longest.

Uses: Garlic is an ancient herb highly valued for its medicinal properties and flavouring qualities. Its antiseptic and anti-viral powers are well documented and it has long been used in the treatment of colds and other respiratory ailments, blood pressure, and externally as a disinfectant. As a culinary herb, garlic can be used as a flavouring for meat, in soups and stews and in salad dressings. Chewing parsley after eating garlic helps remove the strong odour.

GOAT'S RUE *Galega officinalis*

Description: Goat's rue is an extremely attractive, hardy perennial member of the pea family that is commonly grown in European and English gardens. It has bright green, pinnate leaves with eight to ten opposite pairs of lance-shaped leaflets, 2–5 cm long. Classic small 'pea-like' scentless flowers, coloured lilac or white, appear in summer in profusion. They grow in racemes which extend beyond the leaves and are followed by 3–4 cm, cylindrical, reddish pods. The plant grows to just over 1 m in height.

Growing: The main requirement of this herb is deep, moist soil. It is a vigorous grower in sun or semi-shade. Propagation is by seed or division in early spring or autumn and once established it will happily take care of itself.

Uses: These days, goat's rue is cultivated mainly as an attractive addition to the perennial border. Medicinally, it was once prescribed as a cure for the plague, worms and the bites of serpents. An extract of the fresh plant is still used to promote the flow of milk in feeding mothers and it was once said to be 'good for fattening hens'. In France it has been shown that feeding cows this plant increases their production of milk by up to 50%. An extract of the flowers is used like rennet for making cheese.

GOLDENROD *Solidago canadensis, S. speciosa, S. adora*

Description: Goldenrods are hardy perennials of the aster family with narrow, tapered leaves and long, slender 2 m stems topped with plumes of tiny golden flowers. They grow on roadsides and open fields and are seldom cultivated because of their invasive nature.

Growing: If desired, goldenrods can be grown from seed or root division in spring. Plants should be contained in a bed of their own to combat invasiveness. Full sun and average moist soil suits well. Prune heavily after flowering.

Uses: *S. canadensis* and *S. speciosa* are preferred for their blooms while the leaves of sweet goldenrod (*S. adora*) make a healthy and tasty tea. Other varieties are used medicinally to treat a host of internal complaints and externally for wounds, sores and insect bites. The flowers are a useful yellow dye source.

HEARTSEASE *Viola tricolor*

Description: Heartsease is known by a variety of common names including wild pansy, love-in-idleness, herb trinity and in the United States, Johnny jump-up. It is an annual plant producing greatly differing combinations in size and colour of the delightful flowers, but usually mostly purple with different amounts of white, blue and yellow. The flowers are smaller versions of garden pansies and are produced on small sprawling bushes 10–25 cm high. The leaves are small, dark green and heart-shaped.

Growing: Heartsease grows well in sunny and semi-shady positions in soil rich in organic material. Plenty of available moisture in the soil ensures good flower production. They grow easily from seed sown in situ in the spring and will readily self-sow if left to go to seed.

Uses: This herb, dried, is mostly used by herbalists nowadays in the form of a lotion to relieve various skin complaints. In the past it was highly regarded as a medicinal plant for relief from epilepsy and asthma and the flowers were said to be good for diseases of the heart.

HELIOTROPE
Heliotropium peruvianum

Description: Heliotrope is an attractive woody shrub with mauve/purple flowers that have a very strong vanilla fragrance. It grows to about 1 m high with dark green,

pebbled, hairy leaves. The flowers are produced over a long period in terminal clusters.

Growing: Heliotropes can either be grown from cuttings taken in spring or from seed sown in the autumn or spring. They thrive in full sun or semi-shade in average garden soil conditions. They need to be pruned back by at least half after flowering in late autumn to encourage flowering and maintain a compact shape. Propery trained, heliotropes make wonderful potted standards.

Uses: The highly fragrant flowers are used in the making of perfume and in the past the whole plant was employed in the treatment of sore throats.

HOPS *Humulus lupulus*

Description: A decorative perennial vine that grows to at least 9 m and is commonly associated with beer making. The leaves are

Above: Horehound *Marrubium vulgare*
Left: Heartsease *Viola tricolor*

opposite and lobed with coarsely toothed edges. The vine is dioecious, i.e., with male and female flowers on separate plants. The female flowers are at first pale green, leafy catkins which develop into pinkish-green fruiting cones. These cones are covered with yellow translucent glands which contain the hop bitters. The male flowers are pale green, tiny and grow in loose bunches during the early summer.

Growing: In some parts of the world hop vines can be seen growing in waste places, hedgerows and on road sides. In cultivation they prefer rich soils that hold plenty of moisture and full sun. They are slow growing to start, but after the first year quickly cover walls and need to be heavily pruned back each year in late autumn.

Uses: Apart from their commercial use in brewing beer, hops have long been valued by herbalists for their sedative qualities. To this end sleep pillows filled with hops and hop tea is used to counteract sleeplessness. When cooked, the very young shoots taste like asparagus.

HOREHOUND *Marrubium vulgare*

Description: A rugged perennial herb, horehound grows to 60 cm high and forms a sprawling bushy plant with woolly, square stems and smallish, wrinkled, grey-green leaves which are smooth on top with fuzzy undersides. In summer, small white flowers in prickly calyces grow from the leaf axils. The fresh leaves have a musk smell which disappears on drying.

Growing: Horehound can be raised from seed sown in spring or autumn, cuttings taken in summer or division in autumn. A hot, dry situation suits well and the plant will grow in poor, dry soils.

Uses: Horehound candy is easy to make and very effective in relieving coughs and general chest complaints. (See *Herbal Gifts and Crafts* chapter 7.) It is marrubin, a chemical compound extracted from horehound, that acts as an expectorant. Large doses of this herb are purgative and may cause irregular heartbeat, and the juice may cause skin rashes.

HORSERADISH *Cochlearia armoracia*

Description: Horseradish is a member of the mustard family, a hardy perennial that is mainly grown for its fleshy, edible, pungent root. The leaves resemble dock leaves and are broad, lance-shaped and irregularly lobed. In summer, erect flowering stems appear with small, white, fragrant flowers followed by small, rounded seed pods.

Growing: Horseradish is easy to grow in a sunny position in deep, fertile, moisture-retentive soil that is kept free from weeds to allow the root to develop well. It is simply propagated by crown or root cuttings taken in the autumn or spring. Horseradish will sprout from every piece of root left in the ground so it is advisable grow the plants in a separate garden area.

Uses: As a culinary herb horseradish is well known for its use in hot horseradish sauce. Medicinally, it is used to stimulate digestion, as a diuretic and to induce perspiration. It has also been used as a snuff to clear nasal passages and is said to kill harmful bacteria in the digestive tract. A fungicidal spray for garden plants can be prepared from the leaves.

HYSSOP *Hyssopus officinalis*

Description: Hyssop is a beautiful, evergreen, hardy perennial member of the mint family that forms a neat, rounded bush 1 m in height. The stiff, square stems bear narrow leaves 2–3 cm long with clumps of smaller leaves in the leaf axils. Spires of 6–15 small, tubular flowers are formed in summer and bloom until late autumn. Cultivars available include *H. o.* 'Rosea' and 'Pink Delight' (pink), 'Alba' and 'Aristatus' (dwarf). *H. o.* 'Sissinghurst' is a compact form (25 cm in height) with blue flowers and larger, brighter green leaves.

Growing: Grow hyssop from seed sown in the spring when germination will take 7–10 days. Autumn sown seed will germinate the following spring. Divide established plants in the early spring or autumn. Take cuttings in spring and root them indoors or in the shade. Hyssop grows best in light, alkaline soil in a sunny position. Plants grown in semi-shade will be leggy. Hyssop makes a good hedge if planted 30 cm apart and kept well watered until established.

Uses: Medicinally, hyssop tea is prescribed for respiratory illnesses, to combat rheumatism, induce sweating and relieve intestinal gas. Hyssop extracts have shown antiviral activity against herpes simplex (cold sores) and genital herpes. The oil is used in liqueurs, such as Chartreuse and Benedictine. Dried leaves add a clean aroma to pot-pourri, sachets for the linen closet and laundry rinse water. Hyssop is rich in tannin, an astringent and cold hyssop tea can be splashed on the face to combat oily skin.

JOB'S TEARS *Coix lacrima-jobi*

Description: Job's tears could be mistaken for sweet corn with narrower, branching stems. It is a perennial grass that hails from India, where it is much appreciated for its useful and attractive seeds. They develop on the ends of thread-like stems which grow from the nodes of the long, narrow leaves. At first they are green, turning black, then dark grey and finally white.

Growing: Job's tears grows easily in average garden conditions in full sun with protection from wind. Propagation is by seed or division in spring or autumn. The plant will readily self-sow. Spent stalks dry and new ones spring from the base of the plant each spring. As the weather warms, remove dead stalks. In cold climates new seeds might need to be sown each year. Seeds are best harvested when black or dark grey if intended for ornamental use as that is when they are firmest.

Uses: The seeds are nutritious, containing protein, and can be ground into flour for bread. In the East, a decoction made from boiling the seeds is taken for curing arthritis, pneumonia, diarrhoea and, among other complaints, warts! The tear-shaped, hard, shiny seeds are used as beads in many countries to make bracelets, necklaces, tea cosies and tablecloths. A natural hole exists through the centre of the seed, making them easy to thread.

Job's tears *Coix lacrima-jobi*

LADY'S BEDSTRAW *Galium verum*

Description: Lady's bedstraw is a creeping perennial with small, very narrow, soft leaves that grow in whorls. For long periods over the summer panicles of little, fragrant, bright yellow flowers are produced at the end of the stalks. Although it grows wild in many parts of the world, it is not an aggressive weed and is easily managed in the garden.

Growing: Lady's bedstraw grows easily from seed or division in a light soil. A dry, open, sunny situation suits best.

Uses: One of its popular names is 'Cheese Rennet' as the stems and leaves contain a milk curdling enzyme used to curdle milk for cheese. Cheshire cheese attributes it superior quality and flavour to the addition of this herb. The name 'Lady's bedstraw' refers to its use as fragrant bedding in times gone by. The dried herb has a strong, freshly mown hay smell. Being a member of the madder family of plants (Rubiaceae), the roots yield a red dye and the stems and leaves a yellow dye. Medicinally, an infusion of the leaves can be used as a laxative and a decoction makes a soothing foot bath.

Above: Lady's bedstraw *Galium verum*
Below: Lady's mantle *Alchemilla mollis*

LADY'S MANTLE *Alchemilla mollis*

Description: Lady's mantle is an attractive perennial herb with large, scalloped, kidney-shaped, downy leaves and unusual, tiny, clustering yellow-green flowers that have no petals. The plant grows to 50 cm high and

Lamb's ears *Stachys byzantina*

spreads rapidly in moist, shady conditions.

Growing: Lady's mantle grows from seed or root division in autumn or early spring. It also self-sows. The preferred site is well drained and has light but moist soil. Protection from the hot afternoon sun is essential as this plant does not appreciate drying out.

Uses: Old herbalists described this herb as having 'a very drying and binding character' and it was therefore considered an excellent wound herb. Modern herbalists prescribe it in the form of an infusion for excessive menstruation.

LAMBS' EARS *Stachys byzantina*
Description: Lambs' ears is a half-hardy perennial ground cover with soft, furry, silver-grey, classic-shaped leaves. Their tiny mauve flowers are carried in whorls on spikes that rise up to 1 m above the basal rosette in late spring or early summer. Although the flowers are long-lasting, it is for the reflective quality of the silver leaves that lambs' ears are valued. It also has a miniature version, *S. candida*, that grows to 15 cm.

Growing: Lambs' ears require perfect drainage to avoid rotting into a soggy mess.

Very dry semi-shade or full sun brings the best results. Sow seed or divide and replant in average soil in autumn. It also self-sows.

Uses: Dried leaves can be made into a refreshing tea and young leaves can be eaten raw or steamed as a vegetable. The common name 'woundwort' refers to the traditional use of the leaves as a dressing to stop bleeding.

LAMBS' LETTUCE *Valerianella locusta*
Description: Annual salad herb that grows in a similar way to cos lettuce but has smaller and narrower rounded leaves. In summer, plants produce flat-topped clusters of small rose, blue or white flowers. The open habit means that single leaves may be harvested or the whole plant used just before flowering.

Growing: In temperate climates, a year-round supply may be grown by successive sowing from early spring through to autumn. Winter-grown lamb's lettuce needs full sun but summer-raised plants require shade through the hottest part of the day. Friable soil with plenty of organic fertiliser and moisture produces the sweetest and most succulent leaves.

Uses: Provides salad greens when lettuce is scarce.

LAVENDERS *Lavandula* spp.
Description: The family of lavenders comprises approximately 28 species of evergreen shrubs. The short, narrow, furry leaves range from bright green to deep grey and the familiar, highly-fragrant, tubular flower spikes come in many shades of purple as well as white, pink and green. Heights range from 30 cm to 1 m and flower spikes vary considerably in size.

Growing: Crucial to growing lavender well is excellent drainage, neutral soil, full sun and good air circulation. Lavenders are fairly drought-resistant once established, but need to be watered well in the first season. Plants

Above: Lavender *Lavandula dentata*
Left: Lavender *Lavandula 'Marshwood'*

self-sow or can be grown from seed but generally lavender is propagated by cuttings taken in autumn. Heavy pruning once flowering is finished encourages tight, compact growth. Leggy plants should be replaced with new ones.

Uses: Lavender is prized mainly for its highly perfumed essential oil. Dried flower spikes are commonly used in pot-pourris and sachets, both to freshen the air and discourage pests. Medicinally lavender is used to relieve headaches and nervous tension as the oil has a tranquilising effect.

LEMON BALM *Melissa officinalis*

Description: Lemon balm is a lovely, lemony, perennial herb with heart-shaped, pale green leaves that are toothed, deeply veined and

Lemon balm *Melissa officinalis*

wrinkled. It reaches a height of 60 cm when in flower and spreads quite freely. In summer, bunches of small white flowers grow from the axils of the leaves. The plant generally dies down in late autumn to reappear in spring. There is a variety with golden splotches on the leaves, *M. officinalis* 'Variegata'.

Growing: Lemon balm is ridiculously easy to grow from cuttings, root division or from seed. It also self-seeds. Average soil conditions in a semi-shaded spot are best although the herb will grow in full sun in moist soil. Hard pruning a couple of times during the growing season ensures a constant supply of succulent young leaves.

Uses: Lemon balm is principally a culinary herb which can be generously used in any dish that requires lemon flavouring, including juices, jams, salads, fish and chicken. Medicinally, it is used to combat feverish colds and sleeplessness. Oil of lemon balm is used in furniture polish and perfumery.

LEMON GRASS
Cymobopogon citratus
Description: Lemon grass is a tropical perennial clump-forming grass with long strap-like leaves that have a strong lemon scent. In subtropical conditions the clump reaches 80 cm in height.

Growing: Lemon grass can be grown from seed but it is more usually propagated by division of the clump. Care must be taken when dividing as the tops easily break away from the roots. A warm, sunny spot that is sheltered and well drained is essential. Average garden soil suits. Lemon grass does not tolerate frost.

Uses: As a flavouring herb it is widely used in Asian cuisine and enjoys growing popularity in the West. The thick base of the leaves is finely sliced and added to a wide range of meat, fish and chicken dishes to impart a strong lemon flavour. A refreshing lemon tea can also be made by steeping the shredded bases in boiling water.

LEMON VERBENA *Aloysia triphylla*

Description: A dainty, deciduous shrub from South America with long, slightly rough, narrow, pale green leaves. It can grow to 3 m in height, becoming quite leggy if not pruned. Tiny, pale lilac flowers are produced in spikes at the end of branches followed by two-seeded fruit which sets only in a long growing season.

Growing: Lemon verbena grows well in full sun in temperate climates but prefers semi-shade in hotter climates. Loose soil rich in organic material produces the best growth. Propagate new plants from cuttings taken in spring or summer and grow on in a sheltered, warm place. In colder climates lemon verbena needs to be overwintered inside.

Uses: The leaves, fresh or dried, make delicious lemon-flavoured tea which is said to have a slightly sedative effect. Dried leaves maintain their strong lemon scent for a long time so make sweet smelling additions to pot-pourri.

LOVAGE *Levisticum officinale*

Description: Lovage is a tall, impressive perennial plant with deeply cut, shiny green leaves that grow on hollow stems similar to celery and angelica. Umbels of sulphur yellow flowers appear mid-summer on flowering stalks which can reach 2 m in height. In the winter, lovage dies down. The whole plant, including the edible fleshy roots, has a strong celery-yeast smell.

Growing: Lovage is a tough, easily grown herb that thrives in sun or semi-shade. Deeply dug, composty soil that retains moisture well produces the best plants. Propa-

Golden lemon balm *Melissa officinalis* 'Variegata'

Above: Lemon grass *Cymobopogon citratus*
Below: Lemon verbena *Aloysia triphylla*

gation is by seed or root division in spring or autumn. Seedlings should be spaced at 50 cm to allow for rapid, expansive growth. Seeds quickly lose viability and should be sown soon after they ripen.

Uses: Lovage is a most useful culinary herb as all parts are edible. It must, however, be used sparingly as the flavour is very strong. Chopped leaves and stalks can be added to sauces, soups, stews or mixed with other vegetables. After removing the bitter skin the root, too, can be cooked in casseroles. Ripened seeds can be used to flavour bread and savoury biscuits. Medicinally, lovage was used to cleanse the system and stimulate digestion. It was also used as a deodorant by adding it to bathwater.

MARIGOLD *Calendula officinalis*

Description: Marigolds are well known and loved annuals that provide a riot of bright colour in the summer garden. Daisy flowers, singles and doubles, come in colours from pale yellow to deepest orange and can reach 50 cm in height. The light green, oval leaves are slightly hairy and a little sticky to touch. The flowers close at night.

Marigold *Calendula officinalis*

Growing: Marigolds are easily grown in a wide range of soils in full sun. Seeds can be sown in early spring and if left the plants will readily self-sow.

Uses: The petals of marigolds render a colouring substance called calendulin that is used to dye cloth and hair. They can be used as a substitute for saffron in rice and to colour and flavour omelettes and cheese. The healing properties of marigold have been known for centuries, and made into an ointment it quickly heals superficial skin abrasions. Marigold tea is said to improve the complexion and aid digestion.

MARJORAM

Sweet marjoram, *Origanum majorana*;
pot marjoram, *O. onites*;
oregano, *O. vulgare*

Description: Within the three main types of *Origanum*, many different varieties are grown, all with different intensities of flavour. Sweet marjoram is a perennial, usually grown as an annual in cool climates, and forms a low, bushy plant with small, green-grey leaves on woody stems. Its other common name, knotted marjoram, describes the appearance of the small green buds from which tiny, white flowers appear mid-summer. Pot marjoram, a tougher perennial, has a creeping growth habit and forms a tight mat with heart-shaped, green leaves with reddish stems. The flowering stems stand proud of the mat with dainty white flowers. Oregano is discussed under its own heading.

Growing: Seeds of sweet marjoram can be sown under cover in early spring and planted out in late spring. Pot marjoram is easily propagated by cuttings taken in early summer or by division of roots in spring or summer, or by seed. Average soil and full sun suits both species well.

Uses: Both marjorams have a spicy, sweet flavour which has long been valued as a flavouring herb and it is widely used to

enhance Italian dishes, soups, eggs, stuffing and meat. Sweet marjoram should be added just before serving as the delicate flavour can be lost in cooking. The more robust pot marjoram holds its flavour and endures long cooking.

Medicinally, marjoram has antiseptic qualities which can be used to alleviate the symptoms of sore throats and colds. When dried, it was used as a snuff to clear congestion and as an ointment to heal bruises.

MARSHMALLOW *Althaea officinalis*

Description: Marshmallow is an upright perennial marsh plant with oval, grey/green, downy leaves and branching stems reaching over 1 m in height. Leaf edges are toothed and in summer pretty five-petalled, single pink flowers grow in clusters in the leaf axils. During the winter marshmallow is dormant. The plant grows wild in the coastal regions of Europe and Britain and will tolerate salty water.

Growing: Marshmallow can be grown from seed but grows quicker if propagated by root

Mexican marigold *Tagetes lucida*

division. Rich soil, moist conditions and full sun produces attractive plants.

Uses: Medicinally, this herb has been used since AD 700 as a tonic and to treat a host of internal complaints; cystitis, colitis, diarrhoea and vomiting and chest discomfort. An ointment is made from the root to help heal boils and other eruptions of the skin. Although a sweet once made from the thick and fleshy roots of marshmallow inspired the confection that we know today, no part of the plant is used in commercial marshmallows.

MEXICAN MARIGOLD
(Winter tarragon) *Tagetes lucida*

Description: Mexican marigold is a beautiful, useful and extremely hardy herb. The plant forms a neat upright bush 1 m in height with sharply-toothed, dark green leaves. In autumn, clusters of 1 cm golden yellow flowers form at the tips of all the stems, giving rise to the common name, 'cloud plant'. Mexican marigold is closely related to both common garden marigolds and the citrus scented signet marigolds (*T. tenuifolium*). This herb is rarely offered in seed catalogues and is something of a collector's plant.

Growing: Although a perennial, Mexican marigold is often raised as an annual in cooler climates. Sow the distinctive black and white seeds as soon as frosts are over. Seeds take six months to flower so time can be saved by buying seedlings from a herb nursery. The plants grow in a wide range of soils, even sand, in a warm, sunny spot. Mexican marigold grows best in a warm, humid atmosphere, is relatively drought-resistant but appreciates regular watering in extended hot periods. Plants can be propagated by division in early spring or semi-hard cuttings taken in autumn or spring.

Uses: The licorice-anise flavoured leaves make a good substitute for French tarragon and are best added at the end of cooking time. Substitute for tarragon in equal proportions. Dried leaves add fragrance to pot-pourri and sachets. The flowers keep colour well in dried arrangements.

MIGNONETTE *Reseda odorata*

Description: This delightful old-fashioned herb produces loose heads of pale yellow-orange flowers, sweetly fragrant and most attractive to bees. It is a hardy annual, upright, with mid-green, oval leaves which are alternately arranged on square stems that can reach 50 cm in height.

Growing: Rich alkaline soil in a sunny position produces the best results. Seeds are best sown in spring where the plants are to flower. Thin seedlings to 15 cm apart. Mignonettes make good winter-flowering pot plants. Sow seeds in early autumn and thin seedlings to three per pot.

Uses: Centuries ago mignonette was used as a medicinal plant but nowadays it is grown for its attraction to bees and its heavenly fragrance.

MINTS *Mentha* spp.

Description: Many varieties of mint are grown around the world but the most commonly used are spearmint (*M. spicata*), peppermint (*M. piperita*) and applemint (*M. rotundifolia*). All are perennial, spread rapidly from creeping rootstocks, have square stems, highly aromatic leaves and spikes of mauve or white flowers.

Spearmint *M. spicata* Spearmint is the most widely used mint domestically, the one with which mint sauce is made. It is the perfect accompaniment for lamb, baby peas and new potatoes. Mint julep is made with spearmint. The leaves have serrated edges, are closely set, bright green, narrowish and pebbly and the whole plant usually dies back in winter to burst into life with vigorous growth come spring. Upright spikes of whitish flowers are produced in summer.

Peppermint *M. piperita* Two types of peppermint are grown — the white peppermint (*M. piperita officinalis*) and black peppermint (*M. piperita vulgaris*). Black peppermint has deep red stalks with purplish/green serrated leaves, while the leaves of white peppermint are greener with green stalks. Both die back to a few small ground-hugging leaves in the winter, regrow rapidly in spring and produce spikes of mauve flowers in the summer.

Applemint *M. rotundifolia* Applemint has small, rounded, serrated leaves which are hairy and soft and produces spikes of white flowers in the summer. There is a variegated variety (*M. rotundifolia variegata*) with splotches of white on the leaves. Like the other mints, the plant dies back in winter.

Growing: All mints will grow in a sunny spot with adequate water but thrive in a semi-shaded situation, especially given protection from the hot afternoon sun. They will grow in average soil conditions but spread more rapidly in light soil. They should be regularly clipped to ensure a constant supply

Applemint *Mentha rotundifolia*

of fresh sprigs. For ornamental reasons they can be allowed to flower and will die down after that to re-shoot in the spring.

Uses: Traditional uses for spearmint include as mint sauce, boiled with new potatoes and baby peas, and in drinks, both fruit and alcoholic (mint julep). Peppermint is most popularly made into tea, which aids digestion, and peppermint oil is used to flavour sweets, liqueurs and medicine. Chopped applemint gives fruit salad a fine flavour and it can also be used in mint sauce.

MONEYWORT
Lysimachia nummularia

Description: Moneywort is a creeping perennial with pairs of small, green, shiny round leaves. It has bright yellow, cup-shaped flowers. In the autumn, the leaves develop a pink tinge. A golden variety is also grown.

Growing: Because moneywort is not fussy about soil and grows in the shade, it makes a wonderful ground cover beneath trees in damp situations. It is easily propagated by separating rooted stolons and planting. Nipping out the growing tips encourages more side growth which hastens ground covering. It also makes an attractive hanging basket plant for a shady position.

Uses: As a medicinal herb moneywort was infused in red wine and honey and given to treat whooping cough. The leaves contain antiseptic properties and decoctions were applied to superficial flesh wounds.

MUSTARD *Brassica hirta*
Description: The mustards are annual plants of the cabbage family with toothed leaves and small clusters of 1 cm wide, bright yellow flowers. *B. hirta*, or white mustard, is the variety whose seed is most used in prepared mustards. It grows 40–60 cm tall. More rarely seen is *B. juncea*, or brown mustard. It grows more than 1 m tall and is cultivated for its wonderfully, nutritious green leaves. Following flowering, both varieties produce 3–4 cm narrow pods containing several tiny round seeds.

Growing: Mustards grow from seeds sown in spring in cool climes and autumn in

warmer areas. A rich, light soil in full sun with plenty of moisture suits best. Harvest the pods as soon as they begin to turn from green to tan or they will burst and scatter seed.

Uses: From the seeds of white mustard is made the world's leading spice. Young leaves can be used in salads or as a garnish. Medicinally, mustard is used externally as a poultice to relieve congestion and a mustard bath brings relief from muscular pain.

NASTURTIUM *Tropaeolum majus*

Description: Nasturtium is a bright, attractive creeping or climbing plant with large round leaves and brilliantly-coloured, spurred flowers of yellow, red and orange. The whole plant has a pungent smell when crushed and a peppery taste. In some places it can be found growing wild.

Nasturtium *Tropaeolum majus*

Growing: Nasturtiums can easily be grown from seed sown in spring or autumn. Once established they self-seed prolifically. Moist garden soil in a sunny situation is suitable.

Uses: The seeds can be used as a substitute for capers and the flowers and leaves make good additions to salads, used sparingly. The roots exude an essence into the soil which when absorbed by neighbouring plants helps repel pests. Nasturtium contains Vitamin C. Medicinally, this herb is used as a tonic to clear the blood and aid digestion. It is also said to help clear skin and eyes.

OREGANO *Origanum vulgare*

Description: Oregano is the most popular and widely grown of the origanums (see majoram above). It grows wild in the moun-

tains of the Mediterranean and has been used by Greeks and Italians for centuries. It is a creeping perennial plant with heart-shaped, opposite leaves that forms a good ground cover with delicate pink flowers.

Growing: Oregano is easily grown from seed or division of roots in spring or autumn. Full sun and a light, well drained soil ensures good development of flavour.

Uses: Like marjoram, oregano is extensively used in Italian and Greek traditional foods. In ancient times it was used as a strewing herb and medicinally to treat convulsions.

OUR LADY'S MILK THISTLE
Silybum marianum
Description: This is a thistle-like biennial with typical spiny leaves, dark green and marbled. From a rosette of leaves rises 1 m high flowering stalks, sometimes branched, carrying 5 cm wide, terminal purple flowers.

Growing: This herb is not fussy as to soil and will grow in any situation but prefers an open sunny site. Propagation is by seed sown in spring or autumn.

Uses: A medicinal herb once hightly valued for many ailments but most notably for liver complaints. A tea made with the seeds is said to help prevent the after-effects of drinking too much alcohol. With prickles removed the leaves were once boiled and eaten as a vegetable, as was the root. It is said to stimulate milk flow in nursing mothers.

PARSLEY
Curly parsley, *Petroselinum crispum;*
Hamburg parsley, *P. sativum;*
Italian parsley, *P. crispum neapolitanum*
syn. *P. hortense filicinum*
Description: Parsley is a biennial plant with dark green, crinkly or ferny foliage, depend-

Top: True Greek oregano is one of the most popular of the majoram family of herbs.
Middle: Oregano *Origanum vulgare*
Bottom: Curly parsley *Petroselinum crispum*

Pineapple sage *Salvia rutilans*

ing on the variety. In the spring of the second year, tall, hollow, flowering stems appear with compound umbels of tiny, green-white flowers followed by beige, grooved seeds.

Growing: Parsley grows well in rich organic soil that retains moisture. It will grow in full sun but is slower to go to seed if grown in a spot where it receives sun only half the day. Parsley can be grown from seed, although this is very slow to germinate. Soaking seed in warm water before sowing helps. It will self-sow. Use of the leaves can be prolonged by cutting off the flowering stalk when it appears.

Uses: Parsley is very rich in vitamin C. It also contains vitamins A,B1 and B2 along with calcium, protein and iron. It can be added to most foods and is widely used as a garnish. The roots of parsley can be cooked in a casserole. Because of its high nutritional value parsley should be eaten often.

Chewing a sprig of parsley sweetens the breath and neutralises the strong smell of garlic and alcohol.

PINEAPPLE SAGE
Salvia rutilans syn. *S. elegans*

Description: Although part of the sage family, pineapple sage is a different species not commonly used in the kitchen but worthy of growing in the herb garden. It is a half-hardy perennial that forms a very attractive 2 m high multi-branched shrub with soft, velvety green leaves and prolific bright red flowers. The whole plant has a wonderfully strong pineapple fragrance.

Growing: Pineapple sage can be grown from seed but more usually is easily propagated from soft wood cuttings or suckers. A light, composty soil suits best in a sunny position. Prune heavily after flowering to keep the bush leafy.

Uses: Apart from its highly decorative value, pineapple sage can be used to add flavour to fruit salad, herb butters, salads or made into tea. The flowers are edible, can be crystallised, used as a garnish or a fun addition to salads.

PELARGONIUMS *Pelargonium* spp.

Description: Pelargoniums, also known as scented geraniums, are many and varied with leaf shapes ranging from small and rounded to large and oak leaf-shaped. Different varieties have differently fragrant leaves including rose, peppermint, nutmeg, lemon, coconut, apple and lime. They range in height from 12 cm to more than 1 m with smallish flowers of pink, white or lilac. Most are perennial but can be raised as annuals in cold climates.

Growing: Scented geraniums are native to South Africa, specifically the Cape, so need plenty of sun, moisture and good drainage to thrive. They can be grown from cuttings

Pelargoniums, also known as scented geraniums, come in a huge variety of scents. At the top is lemon-scented pelargonium *P. x citrosum*; above is *P. capitatum* 'Attar of Roses' and left is the peppermint-scented pelargonium *P. tomentosum*.

taken in autumn or from seed which do not always come true to type. Most pelargoniums grow well in porous pots although the larger varieties need plenty of space to sprawl.

Uses: Highly fragrant oils are distilled from the scented leaves. Medicinally, most species have astringent properties which make them useful in the treatment of dysentery. Crafters find the dried leaves useful in pot-pourri and cooks use the leaves to flavour desserts and cakes.

Perilla *Perilla frutescens*

PENNYROYAL *Mentha pulegium*

Description: Pennyroyal is a hardy, small-leaved, creeping perennial member of the mint family. It can be seen growing wild in damp places. In the late summer, whorls of small lilac flowers appear at the top of 30 cm square stems. The small, grey-green, toothed, slightly hairy leaves grow up to 3 cm long in opposite pairs. Pennyroyal has a strong minty fragrance, less attractive than culinary mints.

Growing: Grow pennyroyal in a patch of its own or it will take over the garden. It is easily propagated by root division or rooted runners. It will grow in full sun or semi-shade but being shallow rooted it needs plenty of moisture.

Uses: The efficacy of pennyroyal as an insect repellent has been scientifically confirmed. The leaves can be rubbed on the arms and legs to discourage mosquitoes. Centuries ago it was a highly valued herb used medicinally for coughs, venomous bites, liver problems, menstrual problems and as an abortifacient. Taking large doses internally is dangerous. It can cause severe liver damage, convulsions and coma.

PERILLA *Perilla frutescens*

Description: These are half-hardy annual herbs with strikingly attractive, deeply cut, purple or green ruffled foliage that tastes and smells spicy. The green leaf variety, *P. f.* 'Crispa', is milder than the purple. In late summer, 10 cm spikes of small white flowers appear. A particularly pretty purple variety is *P. f.* 'Folius Atropurpurea Laciniata'.

Growing: The seeds of perilla germinate better if stratified with chilling at 5 °C in a moist seed raising mix for at least three days. Plants are frost tender. Provide good garden loam, rich in compost, and pinch out the growing tips to encourage bushiness. Plants grow to 50 cm high.

Uses: It is an extremely decorative plant that looks great in the herb garden when grown in groups. It is also a popular culinary herb in Japan and China, the leaves and seeds being a basic ingredient of tempura. The leaves can be used in salads and also in pickled fruit to add colour and spiciness.

PYRETHRUM
Chrysanthemum cinerariifolium

Description: Pyrethrum is a perennial that forms a clump of greyish, very finely cut foliage from which grow small, white, daisy-like flowers with yellow centres. The flowers have strong, thin stalks and are long-lasting when picked. The plant reaches 80 cm in height.

Growing: Pyrethrum needs light, dry, limey

The petals of old-fashioned roses can be used in pot-pourri and the rosehips of rugosa roses, left, are good for teas, jams and jellies.

Japan and Africa where the flowers are processed to produce the popular insecticide that kills insects without harming mammals.

ROSE *Rosa gallica officinalis*

Description: Many roses are used herbally, particularly in pot-pourri but the traditional herbal rose is the Apothecary's rose. It has been used for centuries in the making of conserves and perfumes because the petals fully retain their fragrance when dried and crushed. The plant forms a 1 m bush with dark green leaves and bristly but thornless stems. The semi-double flowers are deep red with rich golden stamens at the open centre and a lovely strong perfume.

Growing: This rose needs to be grown in full sun in good composty loam that holds moisture well. Deadhead blooms to encourage new buds, and after flowering remove

soil and full sun. It will not tolerate damp conditions or a climate that is very humid. It can be raised from seed sown in late spring or early autumn. Prune heavily after flowering.

Uses: It is the dried flowerbuds that contain the substance used as an insecticide. Pyrethrum is commercially grown in Europe,

dead wood and prune all over lightly.

Uses: Rose petals were, and in some cases still are, used to make confectionery, rose-scented snuff, rose honey, rose wine and vinegar. Medicinally, infusions and syrups were given for coughs and headaches.

ROSEMARY
Rosmarinus officinalis, R. prostratus

Description: Rosemary is a perennial, woody, semi-prostrate (*R. prostratus*) to upright shrub (*R. officinalis*), up to 1–1.5 m. It has tough, dark green, narrow leaves, which are silver underneath and produced in abundance on fairly brittle stems. Small, delicate flowers appear towards the end of the stems in late winter-early spring. Most commonly they are deep blue, but pale blue, pink and white varieties are available. The whole plant is highly aromatic.

Growing: Rosemary is easily grown from cuttings taken in the late spring. It can be

Rosemary *Rosmarinus officinalis*

grown from seed but this takes longer. A sunny site with light, limey soil and plenty of space suits rosemary best. Pinch out the growing tips to encourage bushiness and hard prune when the plant becomes straggly.

Uses: The leaves of rosemary, finely chopped, are popular with cooks to flavour meat and vegetables. Oil of rosemary is used to scent toiletries and rosemary tea was once a popular drink to treat headaches.

RUE *Ruta graveolens*

Description: The aromatic, blue-green, ferny foliage of rue is an appealing addition to the herb garden. It forms a dainty bush up to 1 m high and produces loose clusters of yel-lowish-green, spoon-shaped flowers in the summer. In ancient times it was so highly regarded for its good properties that it was known as the 'herb of grace'.

Growing: Rue can be grown from seed or

Above: Sage *Salvia officinalis*
Left: Golden variegated sage *Salvia officinalis variegata*

gone by it was considered an antidote for a number of poisons. Some people are allergic to rue and it can cause painful blistering of the skin. Nowadays it is not recommended that pregnant woman take rue internally.

SAGE *Salvia officinalis*

Description: Sage is a highly aromatic evergreen perennial with rough, oblong, grey leaves which grow in pairs from square stems. Attractive blue flowers appear in the spring and summer in spikes at the ends of the stems. The plant grows to 50 cm high. There are a number of different varieties grown, among them red, variegated and tricolour.

Growing: Sages strike easily from cuttings taken in spring or can be grown from seed. They need, above all, well drained soil or they will die. A warm, sunny sheltered site

cuttings taken in the summer. It grows well in average garden soil that is well drained in a sheltered, sunny situation. It should be pruned back by one third in the early spring to preserve shape and encourage new growth.

Uses: Herbalists use rue to treat menstrual problems and suppress coughs. In times

The seed head of salsify *Tragopogon porrifolius*.

suits best. Pinching out growing tips when the plants are young promotes bushiness.

Uses: As a culinary herb sage is an invaluable ingredient in rich meat dishes, sausages and stuffing. It aids digestion. Sage hair rinses restore colour to grey hair due to the dying properties in the leaves and acts as a tonic for the scalp. Sage tea was considered a good general spring tonic to promote long life.

SALAD BURNET *Sanguisorba minor*
Description: Salad burnet is a perennial herb with pinnately divided leaves, bearing greyish toothed leaflets. Red flowering stalks arise from a basal rosette of leaves and these carry clusters of greenish-yellow flowerheads; the male flowers have small hanging yellow stamens and the female protruding red stigmas. Salad burnet grows to 1 m in height when in flower.

Growing: Salad burnet self-sows freely or can be grown from seed sown in spring.

Average garden soil is suitable in sun or semi-shade. The plant is naturalised in many parts of the world.

Uses: The young leaves make a welcome addition to salads, cheese and butter. They have a nutty, cucumber flavour. In former

Salad burnet *Sanguisorba minor*

times it was valued as a medicinal herb to staunch blood flow and provide protection against infectious diseases.

SALSIFY *Tragopogon porrifolius*

Description: This herb is a valuable wild vegetable; a tall, hardy biennial with long-veined, reedy, stalkless leaves. The daisy-like, pink flowers are followed by a beautiful, round, golden seed-head, similar to a dandelion. It is most valued for its root which resembles a thin parsnip.

Growing: Salsify is grown from seed sown in deeply-dug, moderately rich soil that has been limed. The plant must be kept well watered to encourage good root growth and situated in a sheltered, sunny position.

Uses: The roots and leaves of salsify are nutritious, containing useful amounts of calcium, phosphorus, copper and iron. Its common name is vegetable oyster as the root boiled, grated and formed into patties tastes of oyster. Young shoots are cooked and eaten like asparagus.

SAVORY

Winter savory, *Satureja montana*;
summer savory, *S. hortensis*

Description: Winter savory is a little, shrubby perennial plant with small, dark green, narrow leaves that are strongly aromatic and white or pale blue flowers. Summer savory is a tender annual with similar leaves and tiny blue or white flowers that grow in the axils of the leaves. It is the better culinary herb.

Growing: Winter savory can be grown from seed, cuttings or division in light soil in a sunny position. Summer savory is grown from seeds sown in spring in a sunny site in average, free-draining loam.

Uses: Summer savory is the classic 'bean herb' recommended to bring out the true flavours of all types of beans. Both savories are known to aid digestion and can be eaten with rich foods such as pork. The flavour of the leaves is peppery so it is used as a natural seasoning in salt-free diets.

Winter savory *Satureja montana*

SEA HOLLY *Eryngium maritimum*

Description: Sea holly is a spiny perennial that looks rather like thistle and is found growing naturally along the shorelines of Europe. The coarsely-toothed, silvery leaves have spiky tips and in summer hard, conical flowerheads are produced, complete with spiny purplish collars. The root of sea holly is thick, fleshy and brittle, deeply penetrating sandy soils in search of water.

Growing: The cultivated variety of sea holly grows well in full sun and good garden soil to which a good measure of sand has been added. To encourage good root development, soil must be on the dry side. Propagation is by seed, root cuttings or division in spring. Sea holly grows best in dry, temperate climates.

Uses: The roots can be boiled or roasted and eaten as a vegetable. Crystallised root pieces are eaten as a sweetmeat. Young flowering shoots can be boiled and eaten

Sea holly *Eryngium maritimum*

much like asparagus. Medicinally, the root was prepared in various ways and was used to treat paralysis, respiratory ailments, nervous disorders and delirium.

SOAPWORT *Saponaria officinalis*

Description: Soapwort is a perennial plant with creeping rhizomes that has an untidy sprawling growth habit. Smooth stems bearing oval, pointed leaves can grow to 1 m long, terminating in clusters of many-petalled, fragrant pink flowers.

Growing: Soapwort likes cultivated, damp soil in sun or semi-shade. It is easily propagated by root division in the spring and it has naturalised in many parts of the world.

Uses: A soapy substance made from the leaves and roots is famed for gently cleaning delicate fabrics and tapestries. It is a simple matter of boiling leaves and/or roots in water, straining and using the resulting liquid to wash the fabric. Medicinally, soapwort is used to treat skin diseases.

SORREL

Garden sorrel, *Rumex acetosa*;
French sorrel, *R. scutatus*

Description: Garden sorrel is a clumping perennial plant that forms a basal rosette at first, then throws up 70 cm branching stems with alternate leaves and terminal clusters of small, reddish-green flowers. The lower leaves are large and juicy (up to 15 cm long) and have long, succulent stalks that are shaped like arrowheads. French sorrel differs from garden sorrel in that the leaves are smaller and wider, though similarly shield-shaped. The whole plant is more fleshy and brittle.

Growing: Both sorrels thrive in acid soils but garden sorrel prefers a damp situation whereas French sorrel likes open, dry conditions. Both require sunny sites. They can be grown from seed or root division in the autumn or spring. To promote more leaf growth, cut flowering stalks as they appear.

Uses: Both sorrels can be cooked as a vegetable like spinach, or combined with other leafy green vegetables to add a sharp, sour flavour. Small quantities can be shredded and added to salads, including potato, as well as omelettes. The leaves may be cooked, mashed and mixed with vinegar and sugar to make the sharp 'greensauce' served with rich meats. French sorrel is the variety used to make the classic 'soupe aux herbes'. In Culpeper's time sorrels were valued for their medicinal properties in the treatment of febrile disorders, tumours and scurvy.

Caution: Because of the high oxalic acid content of these plants, they should not be taken in excess. People suffering with rheumatism, kidney complaints or gout should avoid sorrel entirely.

Garden sorrel *Rumex acetosa*

SOUTHERNWOOD
Artemisia abrotanum

Description: A sturdy, deciduous shrublet that grows to 1 m in height, southernwood has beautiful, grey-green, feathery foliage that stays fresh-looking throughout summer. Flowers, when they are produced, are tiny and insignificant and appear in terminal panicles.

Growing: Southernwood prefers full sun and light soil. Propagate from cuttings taken in spring. Prune heavily in autumn to promote bushiness.

Uses: Like wormwood, the smell of southernwood is disliked by pests so it is used, dried, in sachets to discourage moths.

SWEET BAY *Laurus nobilis*

Description: Sweet bay is a handsome, evergreen, aromatic tree that can reach 15 m in height. It has alternate tough, shiny, 10 cm leaves with wavy edges and small insignificant, whitish flowers that grow from the leaf axils. Female trees produce black, single-seeded fruits.

Growing: Sweet bay grows well in average soil, not too moist, in a sunny or semi-shaded position. It can be grown from seed but is more often propagated from half ripe cuttings taken in mid-summer or suckers taken from beneath the tree. A temperate climate suits best although it will grow in colder conditions with some protection from heavy frost and cold wind.

Uses: Bay is one of the herbs used in bouquet garni. The spicy flavour is strong so it should be used sparingly to enhance the flavour of soups, stews and marinades. Medicinally, bay oil was recommended by Culpeper to relieve pain both externally and internally in many areas of the body. In ancient times the branches were woven into wreaths for heroes and poets.

SWEET CICELY *Myrrhis odorata*

Description: Sweet cicely is a decorative perennial with strong stout roots, large ferny leaves and umbels of small, white, fluffy flowers. It is dormant during the winter but the first to appear in spring and the last to die down in autumn. Several years may pass before the full height of 150 cm is reached. The whole plant has a sweet aniseed fragrance.

Growing: Sweet cicely prefers a cool climate. In more temperate climes, a semi-shaded site with deeply-dug, humusy soil is needed to grow this plant successfully. Provide plenty of moisture during hot summer months. Propagation is by seed which takes many months to germinate, or root division in autumn.

Uses: The whole plant has a sweet liquorice taste and finely chopped leaves added to hot or cold fruit salad greatly

Sweet cicely *Myrrhis odorata*

enhances the flavour and lessens the quantity of sugar needed. Boiled carrots tossed in butter and chopped sweet cicely leaves are delicious. The roots can be boiled and eaten as a vegetable with oil and vinegar. The leaves can also be used to perfume bath water or made into a beneficial spring tonic.

SWEET VIOLET *Viola odorata*

Description: *V. odorata* in the wild is a hardy, low-growing plant with a creeping rootstock above which grows a rosette of dark green, heart-shaped leaves. Dainty, deep purple, sweet smelling flowers are produced in early spring. Cultivated varieties are numerous with single and double flowers in different shades of purple, violet, white, light blue and pink.

Growing: Violets flower best where they receive plenty of spring sun and summer shade, i.e., under deciduous trees or shrubs. They often self-sow and spread readily by runners. Damp, moisture-retentive soil which is fairly rich in organic matter suits them best. Growing violets from seed is tricky and it is better to propagate by division or offshoots.

Uses: In centuries past, the sweet violet was prized as an important healing and strewing herb but nowadays the flowers are mainly used in crystallised form as a garnish. Pressed leaves and flowers are widely used in crafts. Fresh young flowers and leaves can be made into violet tea or added to salads as edible garnishes.

SWEET WOODRUFF
Galium odoratum

Description: Sweet woodruff is a low, mat-forming plant that spreads beneath trees, creating an attractive, dark green ground cover. The small leaves grow in whorls like wagon wheels at intervals up 10–25 cm stems. Charming small, white, star-shaped flowers appear in spring.

Growing: Sweet woodruff grows naturally

Sweet woodruff *Galium odoratum*

on forest floors so these conditions need to be duplicated to grow the plant well. It needs rich, loose soil with plenty of organic matter and moisture. Propagation is by seed which is slow, or root division in spring.

Uses: Dry, sweet woodruff smells like newly mown hay and makes a wonderful addition to earthy pot-pourri. For centuries the plant has been used to flavour alcoholic and non-alcoholic drinks. Medicinally, as a tea, it is said to relieve headaches.

TANSY *Tanacetum vulgare*

Description: Tansy is a beautiful perennial herb with large, ferny, dark green leaves and clusters of small, bright yellow, button flowers. It can reach 1 m in height and spreads quickly by underground runners. It grows wild in parts of the United States and Europe.

Growing: Tansy grows easily in sun or semi-shade in average garden soil. Uncontrolled, it can become a weed, smothering other plants. Propagation is by seed sown in spring, root division in spring or autumn and it readily self-sows.

Uses: For centuries, in Britain, tansy was

Above: Curly tansy *Tanacetum vulgare* var. *crispum*
Right: Russian tarragon *Artemisia dracunculoides*

associated with Easter when bitter herbs were eaten in the form of tansy cakes. Nowadays, it is valued mainly for its long-lasting flowers in dried arrangements and the pungent frangrance of the leaves which repel insects. In Britain it is still used medicinally, in small measure, to treat gout, epilepsy, sprains and to expel worms. In the United States it is completely banned as a herbal medicine and classified as a dangerous drug.

TARRAGON *Artemisia dracunculus*

Description: French tarragon is a perennial herb with long, shiny, narrow leaves growing from slender branching stalks that can reach 60 cm in height. It spreads by runners and dies down in winter. It flowers only in hot dry climates with panicles of small, black and yellow, rounded flowers. Russian tarragon (*A. dracunculoides*) is often grown in herb gardens but lacks the flavour of its true French cousin.

Growing: Full sun, shelter from wind and light sandy soil suit this herb best. Propagation is usually by root division or cuttings which can be difficult to root. Mature plants should be lifted and divided every three years.

Uses: French tarragon is a culinary herb of excellence and is one of the herbs that make the classic collection 'fines herbes', traditionally used in French sauces. It can be added to fish and chicken dishes but should be used sparingly as the aniseed flavour is strong. Tarragon vinegar, made by steeping the fresh herb in cider or wine vinegar, is used to make various sauces and to mix up mustard.

THYME *Thymus* spp.

Description: All varieties of thyme are low-growing perennials with tiny aromatic leaves, sometimes grey, dark green or variegated. There are many different varieties of thyme

but the most commonly used is common thyme (*T. vulgaris*). Other popular varieties include: orange thyme; lemon and golden lemon thyme; silver and silver lemon thyme; wild thyme; pizza thyme; caraway thyme; and pennyroyal thyme.

Caraway thyme *T. herba-barona* A delicious type that is used to flavour the famous French dish 'Baron de Bouef' with its strong caraway scent. It has an arching growth habit with stems that root at the tips and dark green leaves with deep pink flowers.

Common thyme *T. vulgaris* Common thyme is a low-growing bushy perennial plant with upright woody stems bearing small grey/green rounded leaves. Attractive tiny pink flowers are produced in terminal

Below: A collection of thymes including golden, silver, pizza and woolly thyme.

whorls in the summer. The whole plant is highly aromatic.

Golden lemon thyme *T. citriodorus* **'Aurea'** This type is the same as lemon thyme but has a lovely golden variegation in the leaves. It, too, has a strong lemon scent.

Lemon thyme *T. citriodorus* Lemon thyme is a mat-forming type with slightly larger, darker green leaves and similar pink flowers. When brushed the plant gives off a strong lemon fragrance.

Orange thyme *T. fragrantissimus* **syn.** *T. odoratissimus* Orange thyme has the same growth habit as common thyme but the leaves are darker grey and narrow with pink flowers. The orange fragrance is somewhat vague.

Lemon thyme *Thymus citriodorus*

Pennyroyal thyme *T. pulegioides* Another round-leafed variety, mid green with larger than usual medium pink flowers. It has a vigorous spreading habit, so needs space to grow. The scent is much like wild thyme.

Pizza thyme *T. nummularius* A very attractive type with larger dark green, rounded leaves and rosy pink flowers. It grows faster than other thymes and forms a dense clump with a scent not unlike marjoram.

Silver lemon thyme *T. citriodorus* **'Silver Queen'** Similar to 'Silver Posie', below, with a strong lemon scent.

Silver thyme *T. vulgaris* **'Silver Posie'** The leaves of silver thyme are smaller and seemingly sparser than common thyme but bear pretty white variegations. The flowers are a paler pink but the scent is as strong.

Wild thyme *T. serpyllum* This is the 'Mother of Thyme' from which all the other

Valerian *Valeriana officinalis*

thymes have been developed. It has a trailing growth habit with lilac/pink flowers and larger rounded leaves. The fragrance is less pungent than common thyme.

Growing: Thyme plants need full sun, light, sandy soil with compost and plenty of moisture in summer. Thymes will grow in heavier soils but tend to produce less fragrant oils. Propagation is by seed, cuttings or root division in early spring.

Uses: Thyme is a classic culinary herb which, with parsley and bay, forms the traditional bouquet garni of French cuisine. Thyme can be added to casseroles and soups, tomato or carrot juice and vegetables like marrow and aubergine. Use sparingly though as the flavour is strong. Medicinally, thyme can be made into tea to treat colds and chest infections along with skin sores. Thyme is very attractive to bees and thyme-flavoured honey is delicious.

VALERIAN *Valeriana officinalis*

Description: Valerian is a perennial that is sometimes known as garden heliotrope as the flowers have a similar fragrance. After a period of winter dormancy, dark green, deeply lobed basal leaves appear from a grooved stem; the paired stem leaves are pinnately divided into 4–12 pairs of toothed leaflets. Leaves become progressively smaller towards the top of the stem. In mid-summer, flat-headed clusters of white and sometimes pink or lavender flowers appear at the end of tall, flowering stalks. In ideal conditions the plants can reach 1 m tall. The small seeds are distributed by tiny attached parachutes.

Growing: Plants can be grown from fresh seed sown in summer, division of old clumps, or separation of stolons. Seeds need light to germinate. Plants will grow in sun or shade, wet or dry soils and tend to be invasive. Mature plants also self-sow readily.

Uses: Valerian is never used in cooking but medicinally the dried root is used as an anti-spasmodic, sleep aid and calmative. Bitter valerian tea is sometimes drunk as a relaxant before bed. Overdoses may cause headaches, muscular spasms, vomiting, dizziness and depression.

VIETNAMESE MINT
Polygonum odoratum

Description: This herb, also known as Vietnamese rau ram, is a perennial which grows up to 1 m in height. The narrow pointed leaves are bright green at first, but become reddish brown along the margins if grown away from water. Pretty spikes of pink flowers appear late autumn. The whole plant has an unusual fragrance and peppery taste.

Growing: Vietnamese mint is easily grown from cuttings rooted in water or soil or from seed sown in spring. It prefers damp soil near water, and warm temperatures. Sun or semi-shade suits.

Uses: As its common name suggests, this plant is widely used as a souring herb in a variety of Asian dishes.

WORMWOOD Artemisia absinthium

Description: This herbal shrub grows from 50 cm to 150 cm tall with silky, deeply-cut, aromatic, grey-green leaves. Panicles of insignificant yellow flowers bloom in summer after which the entire flower stalk dies away. Two outstanding cultivars with particularly silvery and feathery foliage are 'Lambrook Silver' and 'Powis Castle'. Useful for hedging is tree wormwood (A. arborescens). It grows to 1.2 m and has the same growing requirements as A. absinthium.

Growing: A native of the temperate zones of North Africa and Eurasia, A. absinthium prefers a sunny, dryish spot in average to poor soil. Propagate by striking semi-hardwood cuttings in the summer or by sowing seed in late spring. Prune wormwood heavi-

ly in autumn to maintain compact shape.

Uses: Being the bitterest of herbs, wormwood was used medicinally for expelling worms and as an ingredient in absinthe liqueur. As a strewing herb it discouraged pests and still today is dried, made into sachets and placed among clothing to discourage moths.

YARROW Achillea millefolium

Description: Yarrow is one of the oldest

herbs known to humans. The Chinese recorded the use of yarrow more than 4,000 years ago. It grows wild the world over but mainly in the Northern Hemisphere. It has feathery, dark green leaves with attractive corymbs of tiny white or pale pink flowers which are produced on stems 40 cm high. Numerous varieties with differing leaf shapes and flower colour are grown.

Growing: Most yarrows prefer light, well drained soil and full sun. They are easily

Red yarrow *Achillea millefolium*

propagated by seed or root division in the spring. They spread by runners.

Uses: Yarrow is primarily known for its ability to staunch bleeding, hence the common name, 'woundwort'. It is also used in herbal shampoos as it is believed to prevent baldness. Yarrow tea is said to bring down fevers. The flowers are beautiful, dry well and last a long time.

Chapter 5

HARVESTING, PRESERVING AND STORING

Thyme, lemon verbena, santolina and pyrethrum.

THE flavour and essence of herbs can be enjoyed long after the summer has passed by harvesting and preserving them in a number of different ways. The most common method for the home gardener is air drying and storing in airtight containers, but other ways include microwave drying, freezing and preserving in herbal oils and vinegars.

Harvesting

By observing a few basic rules, herbs can be harvested when their valuable qualities are at their best:

- Herbs to be preserved should be handled with care. Avoid bruising the leaves and thereby releasing volatile oils.
- Gather herbs early in the morning after the dew has dried and before the sun gets hot.

- Harvest and process herbs one at a time to avoid the flavours becoming mingled. Inspect them for pests and remove affected parts.
- Never harvest damp herbs for storage as they quickly deteriorate and remember to use clean, sharp secateurs.
- As a general rule, culinary herbs like basil, sage, parsley, thyme, chervil, coriander and salad burnet tend to develop a bitter flavour when mature. It is best to use young leaves, harvesting them before flower stalks form.
- Medicinal herbs are better harvested in full maturity when oils, gels and juices have developed to their maximum strength.
- Herbs intended for dried arrangements are best harvested when mature.

What part and when to harvest

Plant	Part	When to harvest
Aloe vera	outer leaves	autumn
Anise	leaves, seeds	autumn
Anise hyssop	leaves, flowers	summer
Basil	leaves	all season
Bear's breeches	flowers	summer
Bergamot	leaves, flowers	autumn
Betony	leaves, flowers	autumn
Borage	leaves, flowers	all season
Caraway	leaves, seeds	summer, autumn
Catnip	leaves	summer
Chamomile	leaves, flowers	autumn
Chervil	leaves	spring, summer
Chicory	leaves, roots	spring, summer
Chives	leaves, flowers	all season
Clary sage	leaves, flowers	autumn
Comfrey	leaves	summer, autumn
Coriander, cilantro	leaves, seeds	all season
Cornflower	flowers	summer
Costmary	leaves	spring, summer
Cotton lavender	leaves, flowers	autumn
Curry plant	leaves, flowers	spring, summer
Dandelion	whole plant	all season
Dill	leaves, seeds	spring, summer
Elder	flowers, berries	summer, autumn
Evening primrose	whole plant	summer, autumn
Fennel	leaves, seeds, roots	summer, autumn
Fenugreek	seeds	autumn
Feverfew	leaves	summer
Five seasons herb	leaves	summer
Garlic	bulb	summer
Goldenrod	leaves, flowers	summer
Heartsease	leaves, flowers	summer
Hops	shoots, flowers	spring, autumn
Horehound	leaves	summer, autumn
Horseradish	root	autumn
Hyssop	leaves	summer, autumn
Job's tears	seeds	autumn
Lady's bedstraw	stems, leaves	autumn
Lady's mantle	leaves	summer

Plant	Part	When to harvest
Lambs' ears	leaves	summer
Lambs' lettuce	leaves	spring, summer
Lavenders	leaves, flowers	summer, autumn
Lemon balm	leaves	all season
Lemon grass	leaves	summer, autumn
Lemon verbena	leaves	summer
Lovage	whole plant	autumn
Marigold	petals	summer
Marjoram	leaves, flowers	spring, summer
Marshmallow	root	autumn
Mexican marigold	leaves	summer
Mint	leaves	spring, summer
Moneywort	leaves	summer
Mustard	leaves, seeds	spring
Nasturtium	leaves, seeds, flowers	summer, autumn
Oregano	leaves	summer
Parsley	leaves	spring, summer
Pelargoniums	leaves	summer
Pennyroyal	leaves	all season
Perilla	leaves, seeds	summer, autumn
Pineapple sage	leaves, flowers	summer, autumn
Pyrethrum	flowers	autumn
Rosemary	leaves	all season
Rose	petals, hops	summer
Sage	leaves	spring, summer
Salad burnet	leaves	spring
Salsify	root, leaves	summer, autumn
Savory	leaves	summer
Sea holly	shoots, roots	spring, summer
Soapwort	leaves, roots	autumn
Sorrel	leaves	spring, summer
Southernwood	leaves	autumn
Sweet bay	leaves	all season
Sweet cicely	leaves	spring, summer
Sweet woodruff	whole plant	autumn
Tansy	leaves, flowers	autumn
Tarragon	leaves	summer
Thyme	leaves	summer, autumn
Valerian	root	autumn
Vietnamese mint	leaves	spring, summer
Wormwood	leaves	autumn
Yarrow	leaves, flowers	summer, autumn

Lavender holds its fragrance well when dried.

Drying
Air drying

Leaves, flowers and seed-heads can be successfully air dried in a number of different places, providing it is warm, dry and dark (to preserve colour) with plenty of ventilation and free from fumes and condensation. This could be a cellar, airing closet, attic, garage or specially designed drying cabinet.

Leaves to be dried should be harvested just before the plant flowers as most volatile oils are fully developed at this time.

Flowers should be picked, with the stem, when fully open and bone dry. Heads of seeds need to be harvested when they are ripe (i.e., changed colour) but before they begin falling. If in doubt, seed-heads such as fennel, lovage, coriander and dill can be enclosed in a plastic bag that is bound at the stem. This prevents loss of seed by dispersement or birds.

Most roots are gathered in the autumn after flowering.

It is important that the plant material is hung or placed in a manner that ensures plenty of free air movement. Crowding causes mould.

It can take anywhere from three days to three weeks for plants to air dry, depending on the particular herb and the air temperature. Check after three days and then monitor the drying process daily. Leaves and flowers should be crisp but not brittle to the point of shattering. Roots must be dry right through and if the seeds drop when the heads are shaken, they are ready to store.

Storage time for dried herbs is about one year, after which they need to be replaced.

Drying in the microwave

Small quantities of some culinary herbs can be dried in the microwave in minutes. It is not the most suitable method for all herbs as microwaves can easily dry up essential oils,

but some herbs have an abundance and enough is left to be useful.

Because microwave ovens and leaf sizes vary so much, it is difficult to give exact times, but the times given below worked for me in my microwave. Lay the leaves or sprigs between two sheets of paper towel on the oven platter and process on the 'defrost' setting. I suggest you start at 60 seconds and proceed at 20 second intervals.

Basil — 1 min
Calendula (individual petals) — 80 secs
Catnip — 1½ mins
Chervil — 1 min
Chives — 1 min
Fennel — 80 secs
Feverfew — 1½ mins
Lemon balm — 1 min 20 secs
Lovage — start at 50 secs and proceed at 10 sec intervals
Parsley — 1 min
Rosemary — 1 min 20 secs
Sage — 1 min 30 secs
Thyme — 1 min

Lemon verbena keeps its strong scent well when preserved.

Freezing

Freezing is a great way to preserve herbs intended for cooking. It is quick and easy and the herbs retain their colour and nutritional value. If they are to be used within the first six weeks they can be washed and frozen fresh from the garden. For longer storage they will need to be blanched. Just remember to date and label the herbs, as their freezer life is about six months. Mixed herbs for casseroles can be chopped and packed into an ice cube tray and topped up with water. When frozen, the herb blocks can be loosely packed in plastic bags.

Herb vinegars

Making herbal vinegars is simple and fun because the vinegar so easily absorbs the aromatic flavours of culinary herbs and you can experiment with any combinations you choose. My favourite is fennel, garlic, tarragon and chives in cider vinegar, which I use to marinate steak. Cider, malt or white wine vinegar is suitable to use and a whole range of attractive bottles is available to store the vinegar.

Wash, dry and bruise about 2½ cups of herbs and tightly pack them into a preserving jar big enough to hold 750 ml or 1 litre of vinegar, depending on the size of your bottle. Add vinegar, a couple of cloves of garlic or several peppercorns and tightly seal. Leave it for two days, then give it a good shake and continue to do so every other day for the next 10 days. Strain the vinegar into a bottle and insert a fresh stem of tarragon, fennel or rosemary with red and black peppercorns for decoration.

Culinary herb oils

Herbal oils add that 'je ne sais quoi' touch of magic flavour to fried meats, rice and dressings and, like vinegars, they are easy to make. The important thing to remember is that oil needs heat to absorb herbal flavours, so make it in summer when it can be left on the windowsill for the sun to do its work.

Useful culinary herbs to preserve in oil include thyme, rosemary, basil, tarragon, fennel and savory.

Blend enough herbs to fill a couple of tablespoons and place in a 1 litre preserving jar. Add 750 mls of olive oil. Other vegetable oils can be substituted but they lack the richness of olive oil. Seal the jar and place in the sun. Every day for three to four weeks, shake the jar. After this time, strain and bottle, adding a fresh stem of whatever herb you used to flavour the oil.

A selection of three popular herbs for vinegars and oils — bronze fennel, costmary and borage.

Chapter 6

HERBS FOR HEALTH
AND BEAUTY

Assorted sages and thymes.

FOR centuries herbs have been used in cosmetics to protect and enhance the skin and hair. Today, they have been largely replaced by commercial preparations, but it is less expensive and more fun to prepare simple concoctions at home. Although the efficacy of many herbal beauty aids has not been scientifically proven, their succes has been passed down by word of mouth for hundreds of years.

Infusions

The easiest way of using herbs for beauty is by making simple infusions, that is, pouring boiling water over the chosen herb, leaving for a minimum of 10–15 mins, sieving and bottling. The standard recipe is 3 teaspoons of dried herb to 1 cup of water. At least double the quantity of fresh herbs can be used.

Herbal preparations are organic and will only keep for a few days out of refrigeration. In the fridge they will keep for a number of weeks. Natural antiseptics like lavender will keep for several months. It pays to make small quantities to ensure you are using only fresh products. Use only glass or china for storage as metal may cause chemical reactions with certain herbs.

Apply the following infusions to the face with cottonwool or lint:

Chamomile flowers	Acne, skin cleanser, tired eyes
Fennel leaves	Skin tonic, wrinkles, tired eyes
Lavender flowers	Skin tonic
Sage leaves	Skin refiner
Salad burnet	Skin refiner
Yarrow	Chapped hands, facial cleanser

For the hair

Infusions for the hair should be massaged into the scalp at least three times a week.

Blue cornflowers	Rinse for grey hair
Chamomile	To lighten fair hair, make a strong infusion by allowing herb to steep for at least two hours
Rosemary, parsley, sage	Gives shine to dark hair
Sage	To darken dark hair, steep sage leaves overnight
Yarrow, marigold, chamomile	Gives shine to fair hair

Bath bags

Running the hot water through a herbal bath bag turns simple bath water into a reviving luxury. Sew together two 15 cm squares of muslin or net, attach a string to enable the bag to be hung from the hot tap and fill it with your favourite fragrant herbs. Try chamomile, rose petals and valerian for relaxation, or rosemary and mint for stimulation.

Moisturisers

Four parts glycerine and three parts rosewater (available from chemists and craft shops) mixed with three parts infusion of chamomile flowers or comfrey makes a wonderful moisturiser. Mix well and store in the fridge.

Fragrant oils

Home-made fragrant oil can be made by steeping herbs like rosemary, lavender or rose petals in warmed almond or olive oil. Place the tightly capped bottle of oil with the herbs in it on a sunny window-sill and leave for three weeks. Fragrant lavender oil can be rubbed on temples to relieve a headache, rosemary to lift the spirits, peppermints to energise, and so on. Add a few drops to the bath for a touch of luxury.

The flowers of elder *Sambucus nigra*.

Herbal teas for relaxation

Herbal teas are great for stress but they should be taken in moderation. One cup in the evening is sufficient on a long-term basis unless specifically prescribed by a herbalist. Depending on the herb, drinking excess herbal tea can result in an imbalance in the body, causing harm.

The standard recipe is one teaspoon of dried herbs or three teaspoons of fresh herbs to a cup of boiling water. Allow to stand covered for 5 minutes. Sweeten with honey if preferred. Do not use metal teapots as some herbs react chemically with metal.

Basil	For nervousness
Borage	To purify the blood
Dandelion	Blood purifier and tonic
Elderflower, aniseed, hops	For sleep
Lemon balm, peppermint, chamomile	Relaxation
Lemon verbena	Cooling in hot weather

Chapter 7

HERBAL GIFTS AND CRAFTS

A cloth mouse filled with catmint will become your cat's favourite toy.

THERE is that extra special something about herbal gifts, both for the giver and the receiver. And it's to do with their spicy fragrance, romantic history and the knowledge that so much of the giver has gone into making the gift. From herbs that are home-grown we can make tussie mussies, herbal sleep pillows, closet fresheners, fragrant herbal stuffed toys, mothbags, pot-pourri and beauty aids. (See also herb vinegars and oils, pages 84–85.)

Tussie mussies

The gift of a tussie mussie, or small herbal posy, has special significance as each leaf and flower has meaning and they are especially chosen to convey messages of love, congratulations, appreciation and admiration, or sorrow, sympathy and grief.

Consult a book on the language of flowers and then gather the appropriate herbs.

Start with a central flower, like a small carnation or rose, and build up circlets of flowers and leaves around the central flower, tying in each circlet. Choose large leaves for the outer circle, like peppermint geranium, to frame the posy. Trim all the stems to the same length and tie them together at the base. Cut a small cross in the centre of a paper doily and slip the stems through to form a nice frilled edge. Secure the doily with a pretty ribbon to which you can tie a little card with the meanings of the herbs.

Herbal pillows

These pillows make a really thoughtful gift for someone who is suffering from headaches, depression, stress or insomnia.

A fragrant herbal wall decoration with bay branches and leaves, chive flowers, rosemary, lavender and sage.

Lavender bags are a gift that is always welcome.

Sew dried herbs into a small muslin bag which can be slipped into the pillowcase, or follow the Victorian idea of a small, stuffed pillow complete with lacy or frilled edge to be cradled against the head to relieve symptoms.

To encourage sleep, use dried hops, rose petals, woodruff and bergamot. For headaches, use dried lavender or any lemon-scented herbs. For sheer luxury, make up a colourful decorative pillow with any strongly fragrant dried herbs you like.

A herbal basket with bronze fennel, tarragon and wild strawberries.

Closet fresheners and moth bags

Small, lacy herb sachets hung on coathangers, or actually sewn into a padded coathanger, can scent the closet and act as a moth repellent. It is a particularly good idea for clothes which are being stored.

Alternatively, cut squares of cotton print fabric with pinking shears, put a tablespoon of mixed, dried herbs and a few cloves in the centre with a little wadding, gather up the four corners and tie with ribbon. These moth bags can be used in drawers or stored suitcases. Herbs used to discourage moths include lavender, mint, tansy, thyme, wormwood, rosemary and santolina.

Stuffed toys

Little bags of cheering herbs, like basil, mint and rosemary, can be tucked into home-made stuffed toys to give them special appeal. For the family cat, a little, stuffed catnip mouse will keep him happy for hours.

Pot-pourri

Pot-pourri is a mixture of fragrant herbs, flowers and spices combined in a decorative bowl to scent the home. It's a wonderful way of bringing the sweet smells of the summer herb garden indoors for winter. Combinations are many and varied but the most important factor is that all the plant material must be bone dry to avoid mould. A typical recipe might be:

2 cups rose petals
2 cups clove carnations
2 cups lavender
1 cup larkspur flowers
12 love-in-a-mist seed capsules
1 cup lemon verbena
1 teaspoon of ground spices like nutmeg, ginger, cloves, cinnamon
5 teaspoons orris root

Rub the inside of a large preserving jar with an aromatic oil such as lavender, rose or rosemary. Combine all the above ingredients in

Decorative dyed seedpods absorb and hold the fragrance of lavender well to make a beautiful and sweet-smelling gift.

the jar and lightly stir. Seal tightly and leave for about six weeks to mature. Shake every couple of days to blend.

Horehound coughdrops

This recipe is one of the most popular uses of horehound and is ideal for soothing the throat.

2 cups sugar
25 grams butter
½ cup horehound infusion (made by infusing a handful of horehound in one cup of boiling water for 10 minutes)

Combine ingredients in a thick-bottomed pot and bring to the boil. Boil for five minutes, remove from heat and allow to rest for one minute. Beat briskly until thick and pour into a well-greased shallow pan. When cooled, but before set, cut into small squares. Store in an airtight container when completely cold.

Chapter 8

HERBS IN COOKING

A mix of silver, variegated and common thyme.

HERBS play a vital role in the preparation of fine food. It is hard to imagine a good meal that does not include herbs, either as an ingredient or as a garnish. Our most popular herbs, like parsley, thyme, sage, chives and garlic, are widely used in foods around the world and for that we can thank ancient civilisations. Babylonians and Assyrians were the first to cultivate herbs for food. Romans used herbs extensively in both their food and as medicines and as their empire spread so did the use of herbs.

The French perfected the used of herbs in cooking and today bouquet garni and fines herbs are standard additions to soups and casseroles around the globe.

Bouquet garni is a combination of thyme, bay and parsley. A few sprigs of each is tied together leaving a long thread to tie around the pot handle so that it an be removed before serving. Try always to use fresh herbs, but if they are not available, dried can be crumbled and tied securely in a muslin bag.

The French call a mixture of finely chopped fresh herbs 'fines herbs'. These traditionally consist of tarragon, parsley, chervil and chives. 'Fines herbs' are used to flavour sauces, soups, souffles, savoury custards and all kinds of egg dishes.

Fresh herbs should always be a first choice but if dried must be used, substitute $\frac{1}{2}$ teaspoon of dried herbs for every 2 teaspoons of fresh.

Opposite top: Chervil is a popular culinary herb, particularly in France. It goes well with vegetables, including potatoes, and can be used in soups.

Herbs to use with different foods

Beans	savory, mint, thyme	Marrow	Marjoram, tarragon, thyme
Beef	garlic, marjoram, rosemary, dill, sage, bay, tarragon, thyme	Mushrooms	chives, marjoram
		Onions	sage, marjoram
Breads	coriander, dill, fennel, savory, thyme	Peas	mint, chives, basil, tarragon
		Pork	coriander, fennel, marjoram, tarragon, thyme
Cauliflower	marjoram, rosemary, chervil, thyme	Potatoes	chives, parsley, caraway, chervil, mint, thyme
Carrots	chervil, marjoram, mint, parsley, tarragon	Poultry	bay, dill, lovage, marjoram, tarragon, parsley, sage, thyme
Desserts	angelica, lemon balm, caraway, lemon verbena, mints, borage		
		Pumpkin	mint, chives, parsley
Eggs	basil, chives, parsley, tarragon	Shellfish	basil, dill, lemon balm, marjoram, tarragon, thyme
Fish	bay, dill, fennel, lemon balm, lovage, rosemary, sage	Soups	basil, bay, chervil, chives, coriander, dill, lovage, marjoram, sage, sweet cicely, tarragon
Lamb	garlic, rosemary, mint, sa ge savory, thyme		
Leafy greens	basil, chervil, chives, marjoram, mint	Tomatoes	basil, chives, marjoram, parsley

BIBLIOGRAPHY

Attenborough, David, *The Private Life of Plants*, BBC Books, 1995.

Bailey, L.H., *Hortus III*, Hortorium, Macmillan, 1976.

Berrall, Julia S., *The Garden: An Illustrated History*, Penguin Books, 1978.

Culpeper, Nicholas, *Culpeper's Complete Herbal*, Bloomsbury Books, 1992.

Encyclopedia of Herbs, Marshall Cavendish, 1979.

Grieve, Mrs M., FRHS, *A Modern Herbal*, Tiger Books, 1992.

Griffiths, Mark (ed.) *The New RHS Dictionary Index of Garden Plants*, Macmillan, London, 1994.

Hamett, Dr. Keith, *Plant Propagation*, Reed, 1992.

Harrison, S.G., Masefield G.B., Wallis, Michael, *The Illustrated Book of Food Plants*, Oxford University Press, 1969.

Horrocks, Lorna, *Natural Beauty*, Angus & Robertson, 1992.

Jones, Julia and Deer, Barbara, *Calendar of Garden Lore*, Dorling Kindersley, 1989.

Loewenfeld, Claire and Black, Philippa, *The Completed Book of Herbs and Spices*, A.H. and A.W. Reed, 1976.

Magic and Medicine of Plants, Reader's Digest, 1994.

Mazza, Irma Goodrich, *Herbs for the Kitchen*, Souvenir Press, 1975.

Ortiz, Lambert Elizabeth, *The Encyclopedia of Herbs*, Reader's Digest, 1993.

Painter, Gilian and Power, Elaine, *The Herb Garden Displayed*, Hodder and Stoughton, 1978.

Painter, Gilian and Power, Elaine, *Old and Unusual Herbs*, Hodder and Stoughton, 1982.

Sanecki, Kay N., *The Book of Herbs*, Apple Press, 1985.

Stary, Dr Frantisek and Jirasek, Dr Vaclav, English consultant F.J. Evans (B.Pharm, Ph.D), *Herbs A Concise Guide in Colour*, Hamlyn, 1975.

The Herb Companion (magazine), published by Interweave Press, USA.

Thornton, June, *Make your Own Cosmetics*, Viking, 1994.

Tomkins, Peter and Bird, Christopher, *Secrets of the Soil*, Viking, 1991.

GLOSSARY

anti-spasmodic Remedy which prevents muscular spasm.

carminative Remedy providing relief for flatulence.

calyces (plural of calyx) Bowl-like outer protective part of a flower consisting of fused sepals.

decoction Extract prepared by boiling parts of herbs.

dioecious Single-sexed plants, i.e., having entirely male or female flowers on separate plants.

diuretic A substance that increases the flow of urine.

enzyme A complex protein that causes or accelerates chemical reactions.

expectorant Medicine that promotes the discharge of matter from the lungs by coughing.

glycoside Any compound giving sugar and other products when combined with water.

herbaceous perennial A plant that dies down at the end of the growing season and re-sprouts in the spring.

infusion Extract obtained by steeping the leaves or flowers of a herb in hot water for a given length of time.

laxative A substance that loosens matter in the bowels.

leaf node The stem joint from which leaves grow.

mucilage Gel-like substance extracted from plant tissues, e.g., seeds.

ovate Describes egg-shaped leaves or petals.

panicle A large flower cluster with many individual stalked flowers.

pinnate Describes a compound leaf made up of pairs of usually oppositely arranged leaflets along the stem.

purgative A substance that evacuates the bowels.

raceme An unbranched flower cluster with many stalked flowers borne singly along a main axis.

ray floret A flower, shaped like a daisy, that forms the outer ring of flowers in a composite flower head.

reverse osmosis (commonly known as root *burning*) When concentrated commercial fertilisers are applied too heavily or too close to a plant's root system, the resulting solution in the soil can become stronger than the liquid sap inside the root cells therefore drawing it out by osmotic pressure, rupturing the cell walls and killing the plant.

stolons Prostrate creeping stems, rooting at the leaf nodes.

strewing herb Strongly fragrant herb scattered to counteract foul smells.

strobiles Catkin-like male flower spikes.

tannin A plant-derived substance with astringent properties.

tisane An infusion of dried herbs, i.e., herb tea.

umbel An arrangement of flowers on the plant where all the individual flower stalks arise from the same point.

INDEX